How to Recycle Old Clothes into New Fashions

How to Recycle Old Clothes into New Fashions

Fenya Crown

Drawings by Kristine Campbell

Prentice-Hall, Inc., Englewood Cliffs, N.J.

How to Recycle Old Clothes into New Fashions
by Fenya Crown

Printed in the United States of America

Prentice-Hall International, Inc., London
Prentice-Hall of Australia, Pty. Ltd., Sydney
Prentice-Hall of Canada, Ltd., Toronto
Prentice-Hall of India Private Ltd., New Delhi
Prentice-Hall of Japan, Inc., Tokyo
Prentice-Hall of Southeast Asia Pte. Ltd., Singapore
Whitehall Books Limited, Wellington, New Zealand

10 9 8 7 6 5 4 3 2 1

Library of Congress Cataloging in Publication Data

Crown, Fenya.
    How to recycle old clothes into new fashions.

Includes index.
    1. Clothing and dress—Remaking. I. Title.
TT550.C76   646.4′04   77-4819
ISBN 0-13-430819-0

This book is dedicated to the memory of
Hilda Golfman, who taught me creative
sewing. She was my sister and my friend.

Contents

Contents

How to Recycle Old Clothes into New Fashions

1.
Keeping Up with the Cycles of Fashion

There is constant change in the styles of clothing that we wear. Some of the changes are radical, but most of them are subtle—yet significant to those of us who wish to keep up with current fashions (and changing lifestyles, as reflected in our clothes).

The subtle changes occur in such things as color, necklines, sleeves, and accessories. Sometimes it is only in the way the garment is worn: the collar turned up, the cuffs turned back, or the coat left unbuttoned.

Periodically there is a dramatic change. This may be a radically different length, or some form of nudity previously considered improper—for example, the bikini, jeans that expose the navel, and the see-through top.

To buy new clothes every time fashions change requires a good deal of money—and a tolerance for waste. However, with a certain amount of ingenuity you can keep in fashion by restyling your old clothes. Besides helping your budget, restyling can give you the fun of expressing your creative ideas inexpensively and the excitement of seeing something new emerge from a garment that you were ready to discard. Also, the finished look can reflect your individual taste, not something mass produced.

This handbook is designed to help you do just that, by providing the basic guidelines as well as detailed and easy-to-follow instructions. The ideas in it come

1

from more than twenty years of experience as a designer in the New York fashion industry, which has helped me to remodel many of my own favorite clothes. By following these guidelines, with a little imagination, anyone who sews can create new out of old.

In compiling the many ways one can recycle a tired wardrobe, I have tried to stay with the easiest methods of sewing and the most direct approach to the fashion statement that each garment makes. The purpose behind this approach is to remove the mystique surrounding the designing of clothes, so that even the most timid can have the confidence to try out their own ideas.

WHAT CLOTHES TO RECYCLE

Before starting out to refashion your wardrobe, or any part of it, examine *everything* in your clothes closet, right down to nightgowns and scarves. Separate the things you haven't worn in a year or more. These will be the first to consider altering. If you have a sentimental attachment to any garment, perhaps because of the occasion for which it was worn, put it aside until you can think twice about cutting into it. The same applies to an expensive but little-worn garment which may come back into fashion.

Which fabrics are most suitable for recycling? Almost anything in reasonably good condition (or any part of a garment with some wear left in it) can be used, provided there is compatability in the cleaning process as well as the sewing requirements. This means if you're combining two or more garments into one, all the fabrics and trimmings must be washable, or drycleanable by the same method. In joining together different weight materials, the strain must not be on the lighter one. For example, if a dress has a wool top and a chiffon skirt, the wool can hold up the chiffon; but if you reversed this, the chiffon top would stretch out of shape if it were attached to a heavy skirt. Nor is it advisable to work with fabric that is too worn out to have much wear left in it. Clothes that have cigarette burns or unremovable stains can be added to the recycling pile. However, if the moths got at their favorite diet, wool, the garment should be consigned to a craft scrap bag, and you can cut around the numerous holes and use the material in small projects (unless there are only one or two holes that can be stitched invisibly or covered with a decoration).

Men's clothing can provide interesting additions to your recycling pile. Naturally, you won't cut into a wearable suit or topcoat. But what about the ones that time and good cooking have made too small for the original owner? Jackets, vests, pants, and coats, if the fabric is in good condition, can be transformed into suitable garments for women and youngsters. The material in men's wear is frequently of superior quality and this fact should be considered when you are deciding how to recycle it.

The linen closet can also provide materials for recycling. Pillowcases and sheets, towels, napkins, tablecloths, and place mats all can be converted into attractive apparel. Obviously, you will not cut into anything that you are still using for its original purpose. But articles that no longer match your color schemes or are left over from sets that have worn out—a couple of napkins or a pillowcase; a child's blanket that is too small for the new bed—can become useful again as clothes.

Old hats can supply felt for trims or can be useful in projects that require fabric which can be cut in any direction and does not ravel. Laces, ruffles, and ribbons from discarded lingerie and linens, if still in good condition, should be saved till needed. All of the above will keep you supplied with materials and help with ideas.

Once you've decided which clothes you will recycle, you have to determine what you should convert each article to. A blouse? A skirt? A child's dress? A jacket? In practical terms, the logical choice would be a garment that uses most of the fabric of the original—except where fashion takes precedence. When you are sewing for a teenager, a consultation prior to ripping up a garment will inform you as to whether your ideas are in keeping with the current fads.

Before making any decision, however, look through the chapters that follow for tips and suggestions on the many ways you can update your wardrobe.

2.
Tops-
A Good Place
to Begin

Where to begin your recycling?

Let's start with an item of clothing that has many different versions, each requiring a different amount of fabric. This means you have a wide selection among the old garments to recycle. I'm speaking of the top, which comes in various forms: tunic, smock, blouse, halter, or camisole (sometimes called corselet).

From the fashion viewpoint, a new top can revive and transform your costume from, say, casual morning to dressed-up evening look, even if you wear the same skirt or pants. Tops are also very helpful in creating the illusion of a large wardrobe if you need numerous changes because of your work or social activities. Current styles, as well as your own needs and tastes, should be considered in selecting the type of top you will make.

TUNICS

If I show some partiality in picking the tunic to start with, there are some good reasons. First, tunics have long lifespans in terms of popularity; some version seems to be always in fashion, mainly because we consider this a classic style.

Second, they are very easy to make, usually needing no zippers or complicated closings. Third, a tunic can be worn over pants, skirt, or dress, as Figures 2.1, 2.2, and 2.3 illustrate. It can also double as a dress, on occasion, if the length is suitable.

What clothes can be converted into tunics??

Depending on the style selected, you can use men's shirts, long skirts, old embroidered bureau scarves, and of course dresses, to name just a few of the possibilities. Figure 2.1 illustrates a tunic made from a man's shirt, one that may have a frayed collar or cuffs and some missing buttons, but is otherwise in good condition.

To convert the shirt into a tunic: Rip off the collar; you will use the collarband as a finished neckline, so leave it attached to the shirt. The only seam to rip is the topstitching that holds the collar sandwiched in the band (the broken line in Figure 2.4). For the moment, leave that seam open after removing the collar.

Now cut away the plackets or bands that have the buttons and buttonholes on the front of the shirt.

Trim the excess length from the collarband (as shown by the dotted line in Figure 2.5) to make it the same size as the neckline of the shirt after the front plackets have been removed.

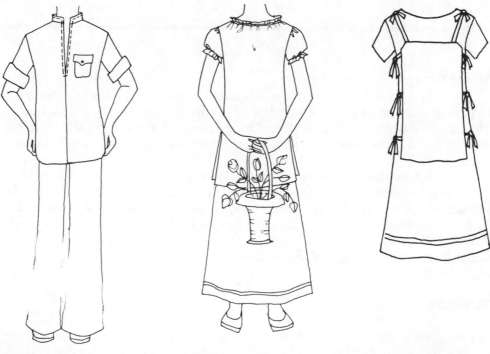

Fig. 2.1   *Fig. 2.2*   *Fig. 2.3*

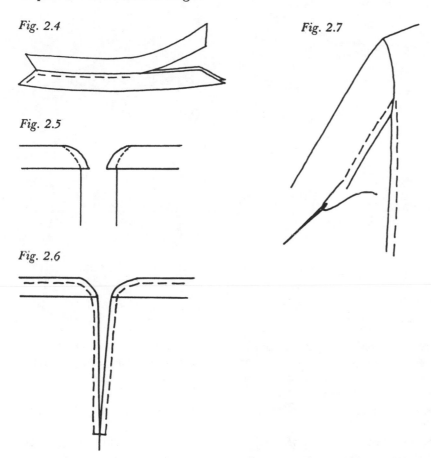

Fig. 2.4

Fig. 2.7

Fig. 2.5

Fig. 2.6

Stitch a center front seam in the shirt, leaving enough room open at the top to let your head through comfortably. Eight inches down from the neckline should be enough.

Cut a facing for each side of the front opening. The fabric for the facings can be some contrasting cloth, or pieces you cut away from the shirt.

To finish the collarband, tuck and baste the raw edges (where you trimmed it) inside as neatly as possible and then topstitch all around the band, where the old topstitching used to be. You can continue this stitch around the edge of the opening after you have sewn on the facings and turned them to the inside.

If the tunic is too wide and the original sleeves too long, here is the way to proceed.

Remove the cuffs and cut the sleeves to the right length, leaving a ½-inch seam allowance at the bottom if you plan to attach new cuffs, or a 3-inch hem if you intend to roll the sleeves up.

Take in the sideseams and also the underarm seams on the sleeves as much as necessary for a comfortable fit.

Fig. 2.8   *Fig. 2.9*

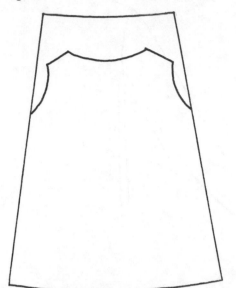

Now you can make new cuffs, perhaps of the same contrasting material used for the front facings. Or you may prefer to finish the sleeves by making deep hems and rolling them up.

Most men's shirts have rounded side hems; if the bottom of the shirt looks right for the new tunic, leave it as it is. Or you may want to straighten and shorten it.

For the tunic in Figure 2.2 the ideal garment to recycle is the long skirt. Whether it is shirred at the waist or flared, there should be sufficient fabric for this style.

Remove the waistband; rip the shirring or tucks at the waist.

Rip open the sideseams, and press all the seams open.

Now you can use a commercial pattern (for a dress or blouse with this neckline and sleeve style) to cut out the neckline and armholes. If the skirt is too narrow at the waist to provide room for the pattern, move the pattern down.

The fabric that is cut away can be used for short sleeves or for bands around the armholes.

If the skirt has extra fullness at the waist, don't cut it away. Instead, when cutting the neckline (where the waistline used to be), make that neckline larger than you need. Then you can run a narrow elastic around the neck and the tunic can be worn on or off the shoulders.

If additional fabric is needed for facings, use lining material of cotton or rayon, or some contrasting material if the facings are to show.

The hem can be finished with side slits.

The tunic in Figure 2.3 is the easiest to make. It is nothing more than the shape of a sandwich board with the underarm cut out for comfort. Back and front are the same.

Instead of sideseams, ribbons stitched on each shoulder, and three on each side under the arm, will tie the back and front together allowing glimpses of skin to show when the tunic isn't worn over another garment.

I made mine from an antique silk bureau scarf, gorgeously embroidered, and tied it with velvet ribbons. If you don't possess such heirlooms, an oblong scarf, wide enough to go from shoulder to shoulder, will also serve. It need not be dressy. A tartan plaid muffler, fastened with leather straps stitched on to hold the sides together, will go attractively over sweaters and other sportswear.

If you are using a fabric that doesn't have finished edges, hem all the sides before attaching fasteners.

Fig. 2.10

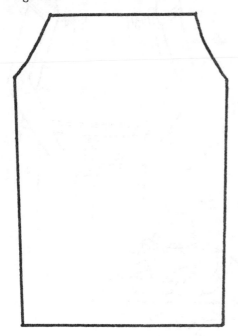

SMOCKS

A smock is an easy-to-wear garment which is cool in summer by itself or can be worn over a shirt or sweater when the weather of fashion requires it. A suitable candidate for recycling into this style is a minidress with a seamed waistline. Or you may use a dirndl skirt, adding a yoke and sleeves made of a compatible fabric (if the skirt doesn't have enough fabric for a yoke and sleeves of self fabric).

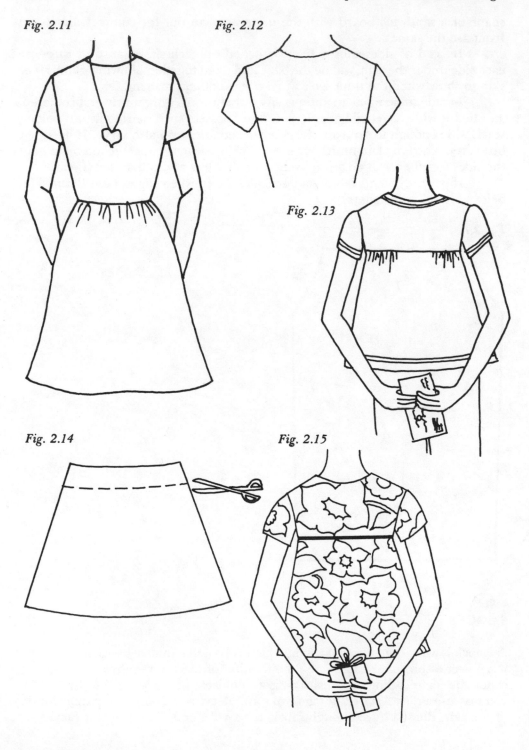

Fig. 2.11

Fig. 2.12

Fig. 2.13

Fig. 2.14

Fig. 2.15

First, rip off the skirt. Then cut the top to form a yoke and sleeves as shown by the dotted line in Figure 2.12.

Do this back and front, leaving the zipper attached at the back of the neck after ripping it out from the rest of the dress.

Release the shirring or darts in the skirt; open the sideseams and press out all ripped seams.

Measure the top of the skirt, back and front, to see if it is as wide as the yoke so that it will fit across from one underarm to the other. If the skirt had shirring in it, you may find more fabric in the skirt than the yoke. Don't cut it away. Instead, shirr the skirt, either straight across or a little on each side, to fit the yoke. Do this back and front if necessary.

If the skirt has no fullness at the waist and measures less than the yoke, you will have to move down to the top of the hips to get the necessary width, as shown by the dotted line in Figure 2.14.

Join the skirt to the yoke with a flat seam, as in Figure 2.15.

If this leaves the smock too short, a ruffle of eyelet embroidery or a band of ribbon or of complementary fabric, can be added to the hem.

Sew the zipper back in place.

BLOUSES

Another attractive fashion is the side-wrapped or the side-buttoned blouse. Garments that lend themselves to conversion into this style include lightweight robes, double-breasted coat dresses, especially knits, and possibly other blouses, if two of them can be combined into one top (see Figures 2.23 and 2.24).

To make the blouse from a robe: If the robe has no waistline, that is, if the whole body is cut in one, without a seam at the waist, mark the waist with chalk or thread.

To determine the waistline before cutting away the skirt, use a commercial pattern (for any garment with a defined waist), or measure one of your garments that has a well-defined waist. (Measure from center back neck seam to waist as shown in Figure 2.17.) Leave a 1½-inch allowance at the waist—½-inch for the seam and 1 inch for comfort so that the blouse won't slide too high when you lift an arm.

If the waistline is still too wide after you wrapped it to fit, make darts or shirrings at side fronts and backs.

The length of the tie belt should be about twice the waist measurement. Fold and press in half the entire length of the belt then fold and press ¼-inch seam allowance to the inside of the belt on the raw edges. Sandwich the hem of the blouse between the open edges of the belt. Beginning at center back, topstitch the belt to the waist of the blouse. This will leave the same amount of extra belting on each side to wrap and tie. Topstitch the seams of the ties. The fabric for the belt can be taken from the hem of the robe or it can be a suitable contrast.

Fig. 2.16

Fig. 2.18

Fig. 2.19

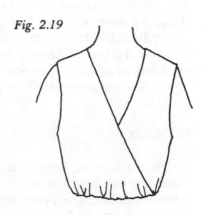

Fig. 2.17

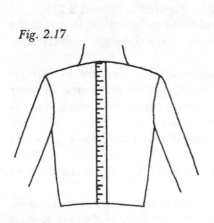

Fig. 2.20

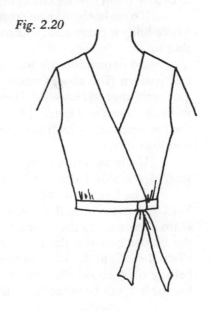

Fig. 2.21   *Fig. 2.22*

Converting a double-breasted coat dress into a belted blouse is a relatively simple job.

If the coat dress has a seamed waistline, use that for your blouse waistline. Be sure not to cut away the seam allowance. If the coat dress has no seam at the waist, mark the waistline from another blouse you own, or use a commercial pattern for any garment with a defined waist.

Cut away the skirt, leaving a ½-inch seam allowance plus an additional inch on the blouse waist.

Open the sideseams almost to the armholes and taper them in towards the waistline as shown by the dotted lines in Figure 2.21.

Cut the belt from the skirt hem, taking only what you need for the width of the belt, doubled, plus a seam allowance. (The rest could make a child's skirt.) Stitch this belt to the bottom of your new blouse.

Close the belt with a pull-through buckle.

Two blouses that you may be tired of can be combined into a new one, provided the fabrics and colors are compatible.

A suitable combination might be one print and one striped cotton blouse. The back, a sleeve, and one front can be of printed material, the rest of the blouse of the striped fabric. Or the combination can be a matter of colors. Two pastel shades can be combined to suit your taste, or you can try a more dramatic approach—red with black, brown and orange, purple with kelly green. Remember to keep your fabrics compatible for cleaning purposes. The entire garment must be equally washable or dry-cleanable.

This can be made as a side-wrapped blouse (Figure 2.23), or the two blouses may be convertible into a shirt style (Figure 2.24).

Fig. 2.23

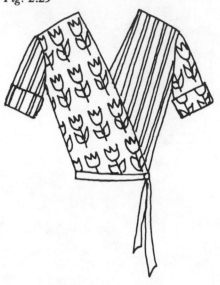

Fig. 2.24

Fig. 2.25

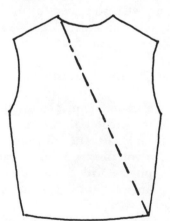

Fig. 2.26

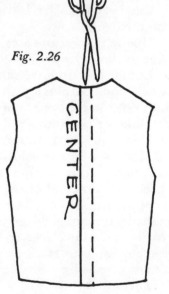

To make the wrap blouse, you may be able to follow the same instructions as for the robe-into-blouse. If the robe pattern is not applicable, however, try the following:

First, rip open the seams of the two blouses and remove the sleeves.

Cut each front diagonally from inside of shoulder to opposite side of waist. (This presumes that each blouse has a plain, one-piece front.)

Face out the bias line on each front with a straight-edged facing so it won't stretch. If the original back had a zipper, remove it and sew up the seam.

Sew up the shoulder seams and sideseams, joining the fronts to the backs.

Put in whichever set of sleeves you want, or perhaps one from each set.

Stitch the belt (made from leftover fabric of one blouse) to the waistline, and face out the back of the neck.

For Figure 2.23, rip the seams of the two blouses and remove the sleeves. Cut each of the fronts 1½ inches beyond the center, to allow for the new overlap. Cut on dotted line shown in Figure 2.26. After sewing on the facings, this extra measurement will give you the lap for buttons and buttonholes.

If the back of the blouse you're going to use has a zipper, remove it and sew up the seam. (The opening is now in the front.) Sew up the shoulders and sideseams.

Put in a set of sleeves saved from one of the two blouses. Add a collar, cut from the leftover pieces.

Make the buttonholes and sew on buttons.

HALTERS

Halters require little fabric and can be made from scarves, embroidered napkins or place mats, and leftover bits of other recycled clothes.

Suitable patterns for halters can often be made from the necklines and top sections of patterns for evening gowns, bathing suits, and lingerie. If you don't have these around the house from previous sewing projects, you might try making ths basic halter patterns yourself. Take some cotton fabric—say a torn bedsheet—to make patterns that can be saved and used as often as needed for the halters.

Figures 2.27 and 2.28 show a halter made out of two large squares. These can be scarves, dinner napkins or bandanas. Cut out both back and front at the top point to fit the neck (Figure 2.33):

Finish off the neckline with a bias tape.

Sew ribbons or strings on the shoulders and at the points under the arms to hold the whole thing together. Some ribbons are sturdy enough to be used as they come. The more fragile ones can be doubled and stitched before attaching to the halter. The strings can be made of contrasting fabric if there is no leftover self fabric.

Fronts

Fig. 2.27

Backs

Fig. 2.28

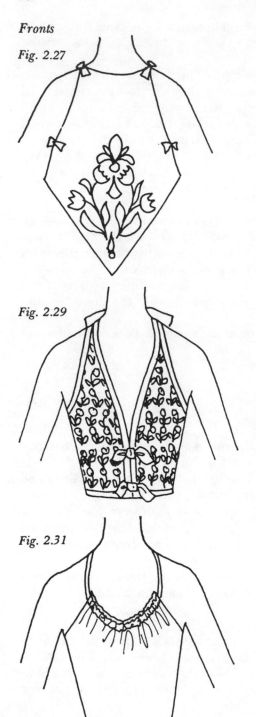

Fig. 2.29

Fig. 2.31

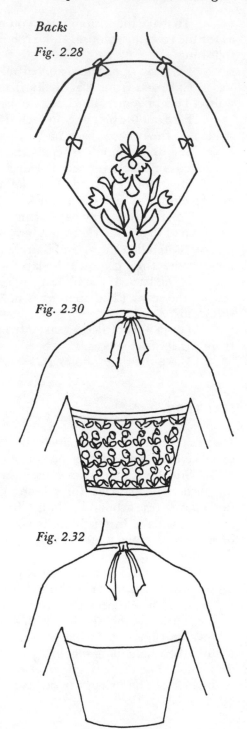

Fig. 2.30

Fig. 2.32

Fig. 2.33 Front and Back

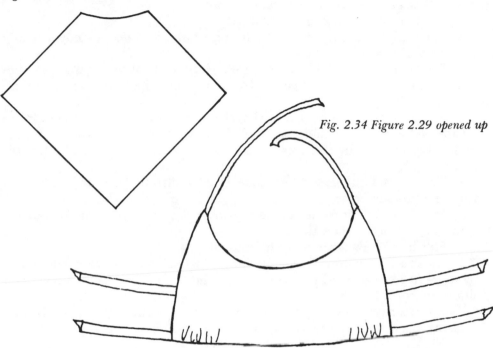

Fig. 2.34 Figure 2.29 opened up

Fig. 2.35 Front

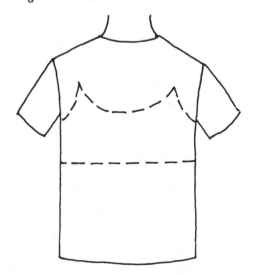

Fig. 2.36 Back

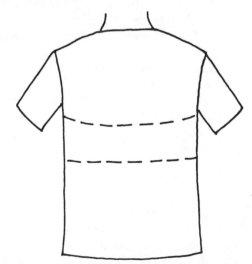

The halter in Figures 2.29 and 2.30 is cut in one piece and tied with strings at back of the neck and at center front.

To make it fit, shirr the bottom front.

Stitch piping around the bottom and finish all other raw edges with a piping or bias tape.

Sew on ribbons or fabric strings (or strings made of the piping) at shoulder points, bottom front, and center front. Tie them into bows to secure the halter on yourself.

The style shown in Figures 2.31 and 2.32 looks attractive in a knit. It can be made without body opening and pulled on over the head. A knitted T-shirt that has become too tight across the shoulders could be converted into this halter.

To do this, first mark the neckline, back and front. Also mark where you want the bottom to be.

Make a casing at front neckline between the points. Also make a casing around the bottom of the halter.

Finish all other raw edges with bias tape.

Insert a cord in the casing at the front neckline. Make the cord sufficiently long to tie in a bow around the neck. Gather the front of the halter a bit as you pull up the cord.

Insert a narrow elastic, cut to the proper measurement (to fit snugly) into the casing at the hem. This will keep the halter anchored in place.

CAMISOLES AND CORSELETS

The camisole (or corselet) is another top that requires little material. This camisole is a shoulder-baring garment, fitted closely to the body with buttons, hooks, or ties. Periodically it becomes the height of fashion and is always fun to wear and to make.

Tops of dresses that were left over when the other parts were recycled can be used here. Of the household linens, I like ruffled or lace-edged pillowcases, if you have a trimmed one remaining from an old set. The fabric, however, must still be in reasonably good condition. You might also have an idle ruffled petticoat or slip that can be used for this style. If the material is very sheer, line it with an opaque fabric.

Figure 2.37 can be easily converted from the leftover top of the button-front dress. If the skirt is still attached to the top, rip it off (although here we're presuming it has already been used somewhere else).

Mark the corselet neckline where you want it to be on you, back and front.

Cut on the dotted line, as in Figure 2.40

If the corselet is too big, take it in at the sideseams.

The new neckline can be finished with a lace or eyelet ruffle. If there are no suitable scraps, the straps can be made of ribbon, which can be doubled if the fabric is not firm enough. Bind the hem with hem binding.

Fig. 2.37

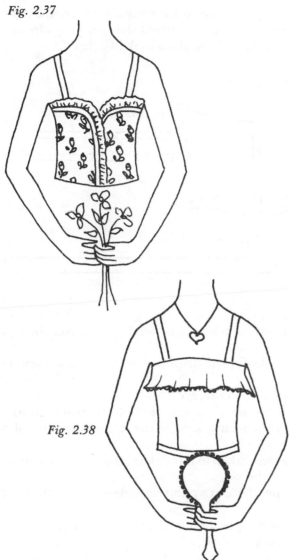

Fig. 2.39

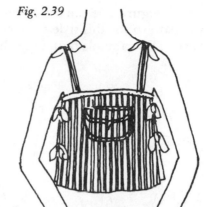

Fig. 2.38

Fig. 2.40

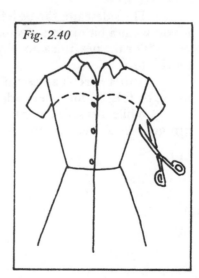

Figure 2.38 can use the ruffled pillowcase to advantage. You can work out the pattern for this style from commercial dress patterns that you may already have. This camisole buttons in the back, and the parts look like this:

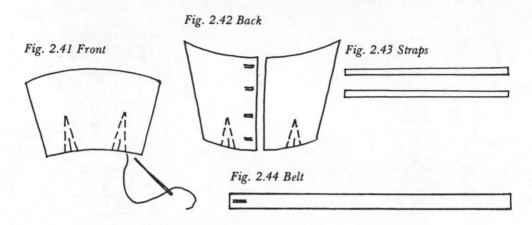

Fig. 2.42 Back

Fig. 2.41 Front

Fig. 2.43 Straps

Fig. 2.44 Belt

Sew up the darts and sideseams.

Sew on the ruffle—ripped from the pillowcase—all the way across the top. Finish the raw edges with a piping.

Make the shoulder straps (from folded strips of fabric) and sew them in place.

Stitch the finished belt around the bottom.

Make buttonholes in the back—one of them in the belt. Sew on buttons.

Figure 2.39 can be made from a miniskirt, or the leftover bottom of a recycled dress.

The sideseams can be left closed, taken in if the skirt is too big, or cut away if you want a bit of skin to show on the sides.

For the ties, use a novelty tape; there are numerous ideas in the variety or fabric store.

If there aren't any scraps for the pocket, it can be made of piqué, patch-work, or fake leather, depending on the fabric of the original garment.

While this style looks like a hot weather idea, if made from a wool plaid it can go over a sweater and add warmth and novelty to a fall costume.

3.
Skirts-
A Reliable Classic

Skirts come periodically to the forefront of the fashion scene. They have a softness and variety of styling that some people find missing in pants. So in checking your clothes that haven't been worn for a while, pick out the ones that will have enough material for a skirt. These can be robes, lightweight coats, capes, and household linens. In this group also there may be some minidresses. But put aside the ones most likely to return to fashion favor—such things happen; save the briefest of them to show your grandchildren how daring you were; convert the others, where possible, into skirts.

SKIRTS FROM MINIDRESSES

Figure 3.1 shows an A-line minidress with sleeves. If the sleeves are wrist-length, they will be about as long as the dress.

Before you proceed, you should measure your hips—and the fabric in the dress, including the sleeves—to make sure you will have enough material. (The sleeves will be converted into side panels in the skirt.) To measure the fabric, run the tape measure from the top of one armhole across the front of the dress to the top of the other armhole. Do the same with the back of the dress and both

Fig. 3.1

sleeves. Add up the total width you can get by joining all the pieces; if it is 3 inches greater than your hip measurement, you can safely proceed to convert it into a skirt.

Rip all the seams and any darts.

Press them out.

You will have pieces that look like this:

Fig. 3.2 Front   *Fig. 3.3 Back*   *Fig. 3.4 Sleeve*   *Fig. 3.5 Sleeve*

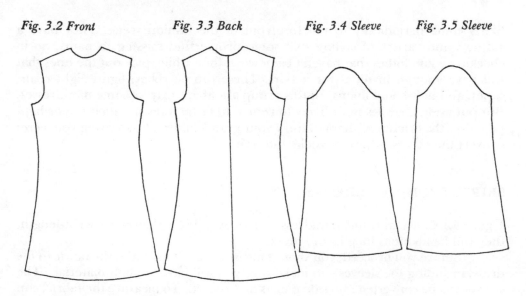

Using a commercial skirt pattern to help you get the correct shape, first change the neckline and armhole seams:

Fig. 3.6 Back and Front   *Fig. 3.7 Sleeves*

Cut where indicated by the dotted lines in Figures 3.6 and 3.7, trying to get the maximum width and length possible.

Now you can join your side panels (made from the sleeves) and get the result shown in figure 3.8. There will be no sideseams, only two side front and two side back seams.

The waistline will be too big. If you want a fitted skirt without tucks or shirring, you must fit the pieces with a commercial pattern in your size before joining them.

The easiest way to make the skirt, however, is to join the four pieces, leaving the excess width in the waistline. Then make an inside tubing at the waist, using a lining material if there isn't enough self fabric to turn back the top. Insert an elastic, cut to your size; or you can use a novelty drawstring pulled through the tubing. Leave an opening at the top of one of the front seams for the drawstring to emerge. Tie to fit your waist.

Fig. 3.8   *Fig. 3.9*

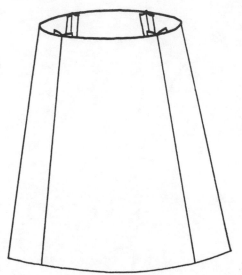

The drawstring can be a hemp cord, yarn braided in several colors, or ribbon for decorative effect.

Another advantage of finishing the waistline this way is that it doesn't require a zipper and there is not too much gather to give excessive bulk.

SKIRTS FROM ROBES

If you have a wrap robe that is still in good condition but has been put aside because it may not suit your idea of comfort—perhaps it was a gift and did not fit comfortably, or the fabric isn't washable and you want all your home clothes to go into the washing machine—this may be the time to turn it into a skirt.

If the robe is seamed at the waistline, rip the seam to separate the top from the bottom. Then rip open the sideseams. If the robe has no waist seam but is cut all in one from shoulder to hem, rip all the seams.

Use a commercial pattern for a wrap skirt to cut out the pieces. If you don't have one, it is very easy to convert a basic back-and-front skirt pattern into a sidewrap. Simply cut one back and two fronts if you are making your skirt wrapped in front. Cut one front and two backs if you want your skirt to lap in the back.

The two edges that will remain open should have the hip curve cut away so that the edges will be straight.

Fold back the edge of the top overlap 2 inches to make a facing. The inner underlap needs only a ½-inch seam.

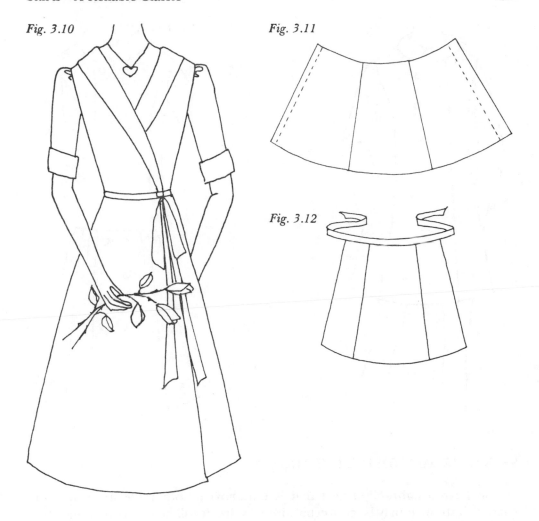

Fig. 3.10

Fig. 3.11

Fig. 3.12

Attach a narrow sash, folded to sandwich the seam allowance, at the waist of the skirt. The sash should be finished at the tie ends (Figure 3.12).

Make an opening in the sash above one of the sideseams so that the tie can be pulled through.

Here is another suggestion for making use of old robes.

If they are too worn to be usable for the outside of the skirt. they may make attractive linings for wrap skirts. The fabric must not be too worn, of course, perhaps mostly faded. Again, watch that the top skirt cloth and the lining can be cleaned by the same process.

This style can benefit from a pretty lining because the open end of the skirt tends to swing away with body movement.

Fig. 3.13

Fig. 3.14

Fig. 3.15

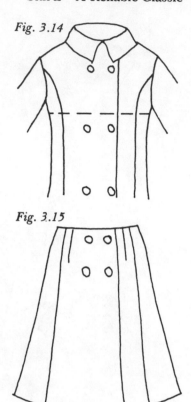

SKIRTS FROM LIGHTWEIGHT COATS

If you have a lightweight coat that is too short or otherwise unsuitable for current fashion, it may be convertible into a skirt. It will be especially effective if the coat is double-breasted.

To see if you have enough length and width for the skirt, first measure the length from the bottom of the armhole to the hem of the coat. Next, measure the width of that part of the coat which will be at the hips as a skirt. This should be about 3 inches below the underarms. Leave the coat buttoned when measuring.

If the measurements are sufficient, rip out the lining, if any, and cut across back and front from the bottom of one armhole to the other, as shown by the dotted line in figure 3.14.

The cut line will become the waistline. This line will be too wide and will require darts or taking in at the seams to fit your waist. Use a commercial skirt pattern if you need help in placing the darts or in judging the extra amount to take into the seams.

If the coat has a deep hem, some of it can be cut away to make the waistband. Otherwise, a grosgrain or velvet ribbon stitched to a stiff backing can be used.

The coat will probably have pockets in the sideseams. These will now be too low for comfort. You can either move them higher up on the seam or remove them and sew up the seams. Since the pockets were in the seams, there will be no marks left on the outside of the fabric. I don't recommend cutting into the remaining parts of the coat—the sleeves and top—since they may provide an interesting yoke and sleeves for some other garment.

SKIRTS FROM CAPES

Most capes have some flare, so if you want a flared skirt, you might consider converting an unused cape into a fashionable skirt. Cut away the top of the shoulders and the neckline. Use a commercial skirt pattern to get the proper fit for the waist and hips. If the cape buttons down the front, keep that as the closing for the skirt, otherwise use a zipper.

SKIRTS FROM HOUSEHOLD LINENS

You might not think of unused embroidered tablecloths or attractive printed sheets in terms of clothing, but both can be made into interesting long skirts. Here, again, I'm not suggesting that expensive household linens be cut up. But there are instances where a topsheet remains while the bottom one has ripped apart, or a tablecloth takes hours to iron and is therefore never used. (You might not mind ironing a new skirt that you can wear frequently.) If most of your

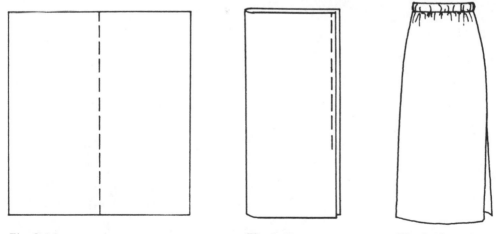

Fig. 3.16   Fig. 3.17   Fig. 3.18

linens are white, there are easy-to-use household dyes that can supply the colors you want.

The simplest way to make a long skirt is first to measure around your hips and the length from your waist to the floor.

Allowing an additional 2 inches in the width and 2 inches in the length, cut an oblong piece of cloth from a tablecloth or printed sheet.

Fold it in the center (the dotted line in Figure 3.16); then bring the two long sides together and sew down to where the knees will be, leaving a slit to the hem (Figure 3.18). Make a casing at the top and insert an elastic that fits your waist.

Make a hem at the bottom, and face out the open side.

HOW TO LENGTHEN SKIRTS

When you lengthen a skirt that is too short, it is important to provide the look of current style rather than just a dropped hemline. Lengthening from the top —that is, putting a yoke on the skirt—will generally accomplish this.

First, remove the waistband (if any) and zipper.

Rip the sideseams.

Using the top of the skirt as a guide for fit, make a paper pattern for a yoke, allowing a ½-inch seam both on the yoke and on the skirt where they will be joined. The yoke can be straight across or shaped, depending on your sewing skills and also on what looks right with the body of the skirt.

The fabric for the yoke can be the same as the body of the skirt if you're converting a dress into a skirt, or if there is some companion garment that can be cut up. However, if you don't have the same fabric, a contrast can serve just as well. For example, a wool skirt will look attractive with a fake leather or suede yoke. (Bear in mind the cleaning compatibility.) For a cotton garment you have a

Fig. 3.19   *Fig. 3.20*   *Fig. 3.21*

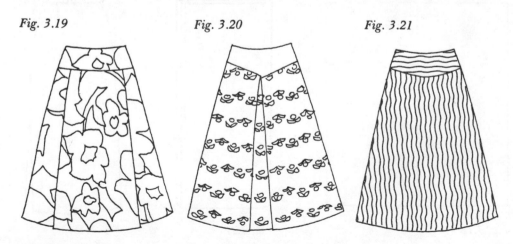

Fig. 3.22   *Fig. 3.23*

wide choice of materials, such as piqué, denim, or gingham. These make interesting yokes for either solid or printed skirts. For knit garments, a knit yoke is suitable. However, lining the yoke with a nonstretchable fabric before attaching it to a skirt will keep the yoke in shape. If you include crochet and knitting among your craft skills, you can knit or crochet a yoke, put it on a lining, and attach it to a skirt for a very individual look.

Another way of adding length to a skirt is to insert bands, either flat or ruffled, into the skirt.

Figure 3.22 is a tailored version with bands of fake suede.

In Figure 3-32 two old cotton skirts—one striped and one flowered—were cut up to create a new skirt. Solid colors that go well together, in color and texture, can also be used.

For either of these:

Rip all seams and press them flat. Before cutting, decide how long you want the new skirt to be. This will help you determine how deep to make the bands. Having done this, mark off the front and back of the skirt where you want to insert the alternating bands.

Cut the bands that will go at the bottom of the skirt a little deeper than the top ones. This will provide a more graceful and flattering look. If all the bands are of even depth, there is an optical illusion of a stumpy body.

Allow ½-inch seams, top and bottom, on each band. After inserting the bands, press the seams open.

If after considering all the above suggestions, you feel that letting the hem down will solve your problem, but you don't like the mark it will leave, here is one more tip.

Fig. 3.24   *Fig. 3.25*

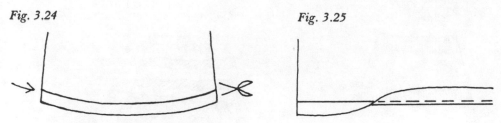

Rip the hem and press flat.

Cut off the hem along the old fold mark (Figure 3.24).

Now sew the hem back again onto the skirt using a ¼-inch seam. Press the seam down on the wrong side (Figure 3.25).

This will give you a couture look of self-binding.

If there isn't enough material to turn up a hem, use a strip of lining material to make a false hem.

Before cutting, decide how long you want the new skirt to be. This will help you determine how deep to make the bands. Having done this, mark off on the front and back of the skirt, where you want to insert the alternating bands.

SHORTENING SKIRTS

Picking up the hem to shorten a skirt may be unsuitable if this will eliminate an attractive border or flare.

An alternate method is to raise the skirt at the belt line or somewhere between the waist and the hem. If the fabric is printed or patterned, raising the skirt at the waist is recommended.

Remove the waistband, measure the skirt, and cut off at the top the required number of inches, leaving a ½-inch seam (Figure 3.26).

Fig. 3.26   *Fig. 3.27*

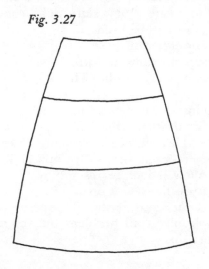

Refit the waistline to your measurements. Do this with tucks or shirrings, or by taking larger seams in the skirt. Replace the waistband.

If the skirt is a solid color without pattern, my favorite way of shortening is to cut two or three horizontal seams into it.

Cut the skirt into tiers, making the bottom tier the widest. Cut away whatever length you don't want—a little from each tier. Be sure to allow a ½-inch seam allowance, top and bottom, on all cut sections. Join the tiers and press seams open on the wrong side.

For a straight skirt, where the lines won't get distorted, the easiest method of shortening, of course, is simply to cut off the amount desired, allowing 2 inches for a new hem.

WIDENING SKIRTS

If you need a little extra width, whether to make a skirt comfortable or to change a slim style into a dirndl, here are a few tips for accomplishing this restyling.

To widen skirts slightly, narrow strips of fabric can be inserted lengthwise. A contrast in color and texture is good, such as satin inserts into crepe, or velveteen into wool, as long as cleaning compatibility is maintained. The insert fabrics can be stitched to the skirt back and front with narrow seams, or top-stitched to the back and front by folding back a narrow seam.

A dressy slim skirt can have a couple of inches added to it with a ribbon placed into each sideseam.

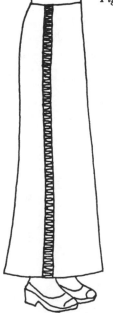

Fig. 3.28 Side View

Fig. 3.29

Fig. 3.30

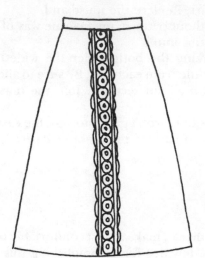

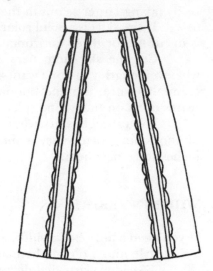

Fig. 3.31

Fig. 3.32

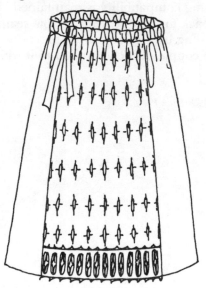

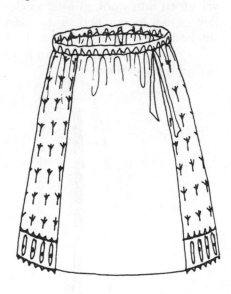

Rip off the waistband and open the sideseams.

Insert grosgrain or velvet ribbon. Since ribbons have finished edges, you can sew them on top of the skirt fabric instead of putting the two edges together on the wrong side as you would with a regular seam. Basting the ribbon to the skirt first will ensure that it is firmly attached and will enable you to topstitch close to the edge of the ribbon. The underneath seam of the skirt, under the ribbon, should be ⅜ inch wide so as not to pull out.

Replace the waistband. This will create a tuxedo look, very effective on a dressy skirt.

For a casual skirt, a commercial trim (such as embroidery) sewn into the center or the two side fronts is suitable.

Figure 3-29 shows one row of trim set into a slashed center front.

Figure 3.30 allows a bit more width because of two insertions, one on each side front.

Both skirts had their waistbands removed before the skirts were cut open. The waistbands were replaced after the trims were sewn in.

The waistbands for all widened skirts have to be enlarged also. Most waistbands have an overlap at the closing. This extra material can be used to make them larger; the ends can simply meet and hook together rather than overlap.

If you wish to make the trimming a more integral part of the skirt, try using the same trim for the waistband or edging the hem.

To alter a fitted skirt into a dirndl or partly shirred skirt you will need at least one wide panel. For cotton skirts, the panels can be made of embroidered or printed cotton towels and pillowcases. You may have remnants from other sewing projects that have enough fabric for panels. Allover cotton laces or contrasting colors can be considered. Only those pieces that are long enough to go from waist to hem should be used. If set in the center front of the skirt, it will create an apron effect.

Panels can also be set into the sides or alternating around the skirt.

The only guide you need is proper measurement so that all the panels end up where you want them and are evenly spaced.

SKIRT POCKETS

For skirts that have nothing wrong with them basically, but could use a little livening up, the following illustrations of pockets may be helpful.

Figure 3.33. Multicolored pocket.

Figure 3.34. Three pockets of checks and stripes set partly into one another.

Figure 3.35. Shirred calico print with ribbon trim.

Figure 3-36. Side pockets with lace ruffles.

Fig. 3.33

Fig. 3.35

Fig. 3.34

Fig. 3.36

4.
Pants and
Their Variations

The first time I wore pants—actually a trouser suit—was in the early Thirties. As a fashion-conscious teenager, determined to become a designer, I followed the styles favored by Hollywood stars. In those days they greatly influenced what was being worn.

A few weeks later Marlene Dietrich was photographed in a pants suit, I completed my version of a white flannel, double-breasted blazer and matching pants. I must confess that in the city where I lived at that time there wasn't another woman to be seen wearing a pants suit, so I can't say the style swept the country, even if my suit did stop some traffic.

But I do wish I had it now. It would require very few adjustments to be in fashion.

The main changes in pants usually concern the length, width, and shape of the leg—that is, whether the trousers are tapered towards the ankles, flared away from the ankles, or hanging straight. Some fashion variations also occur in the upper part of the pants. They may rise to the waist, sit on the hips, or have different types of pockets and closures.

However, if the legs reflect the current trend, the pants will usually look contemporary.

ALTERING STRAIGHT LEGS INTO FLARES

If you want to alter straight bottoms into flares, either of the following two methods will do it for you.

Open the outside seams of the legs below the knees (Figure 4.1) and insert a triangle of some suitable fabric. (Figure 4.2). Leave seam allowance on the sides and hem allowance on the bottom of the triangle.

If you don't have matching material, a contrast can do very well. For example, a striped denim or a bandana print will go with blue jeans. Or an insert of checked gingham can be put in white slacks. Bright plaids or a strong solid color—e.g., a marine blue or tangerine—can also be effective with white.

If the method doesn't work for the particular trousers you want to alter, try the following:

Cut off the legs a couple of inches below the knees.

Using a commercial pattern for flared legs, sew on new bottoms to the pants.

If it becomes necessary to use a different fabric, consider fake suede, leather, or a print. These will combine with most trouser cloths and add a special look to your recycled pants. Figure 4.3 shows the new print bottoms sewn on in

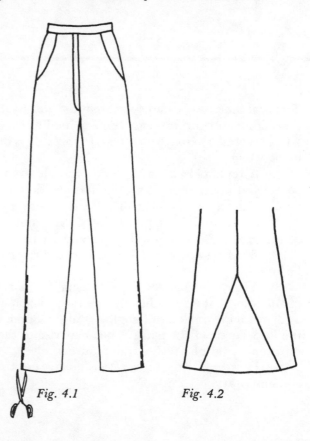

Fig. 4.1   *Fig. 4.2*

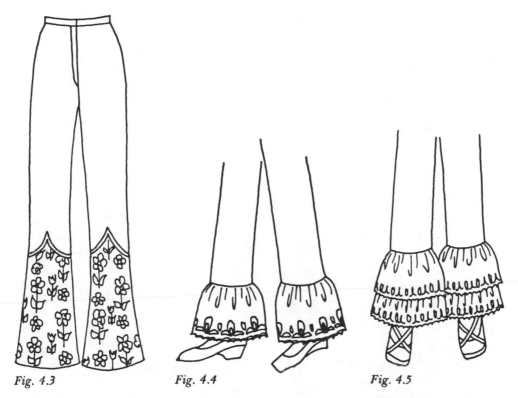

Fig. 4.3   *Fig. 4.4*   *Fig. 4.5*

points, but you can design your own style, as long as you remember to leave a ½-inch seam allowance on top and a hem allowance (about 2 inches) at the bottom.

There are other types of wide bottoms that you can fashion.

Figures 4.4 and 4.5 show ruffled bottoms suitable for patio summer wear. These are periodically fashionable and can be made of eyelet embroidered cotton or lace if the rest of the pants are of a lightweight material. After shirring the ruffle to fit the circumference of the trouser leg, join the two seams on the wrong side, being careful to distribute the fullness equally all around.

CHANGING FLARES TO STRAIGHT LEGS

To change the leg bottoms from flare to straight, you will also start by opening the seams from the knees down.

Some ready-made pants have a slight flare on the inside as well as on the outside seam of the leg. Check the grain of the fabric to see if that applies to the pants you wish to alter. If so, rip open both the inner and outer seams from the knee down. If the grain is straight on the inner seam, then there is no flare on the inside; in this case rip only the outer seam.

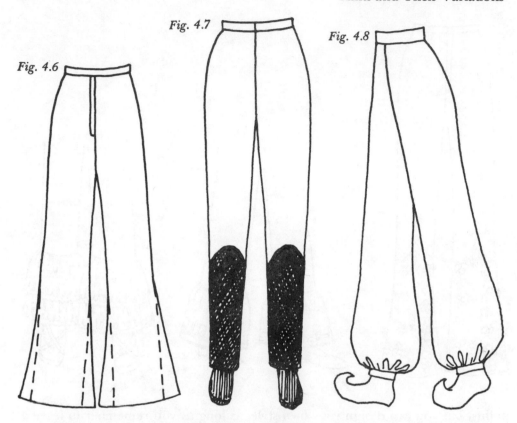

Following the grain, baste a straight line from knee to hem on the seams that were ripped.

Try on the pants before cutting off the flare, to make sure that this method works with your pants. If the result looks the way you want it to, stitch up the seams. If, for some reason, the fit or the look doesn't come up to expectations, there are other ways of altering the flare.

You can cut off the pants leg below the knee and put on new straight bottoms. Figure 4.7 shows new straight bottoms that have the look of boot tops. Fake suede or leather would reinforce this look.

OTHER BOTTOMS FOR PANTS

If the fabric is soft and flowing, you can alter the wide bottoms by putting an elastic into each hem around the ankle, creating a harem look. The elastic should be cut to fit your ankle snugly, and the hem of the pants should be slightly wider than the elastic for easy insertion. A safety pin can thread the elastic through a small opening in the hem which can be sewn up after the two ends of the elastic are joined together.

ALTERING PANTS INTO SHORTER STYLES

A completely new appearance can be achieved by altering the length of the legs rather than the shape.

This is much easier to do, so when a pair of pants is too difficult to reshape, consider what other lengths will be useful to you. If you have been wearing pants that practically sweep the ground, roll up the bottoms to midcalf or higher and see at what point of the leg the look suits you best. Regardless whether the pants are flared or straight, there will be enough material to make a cuffed hem.

This style can be varied by using a contrasting fabric for the cuffs.

Or the cuffs can be eliminated altogether and the hems kept plain.

Most slacks can be turned into shorts of different lengths: Bermudas, just above the knees (Figure 4.10); Jamaicas, midthigh (Figure 4.11); and the short shorts, which go up as high as you can cut them (Figure 4.12).

Fig. 4.9

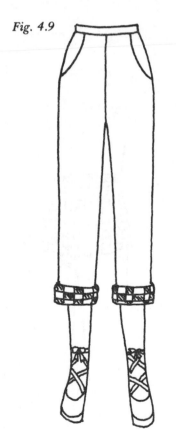

Fig. 4.10

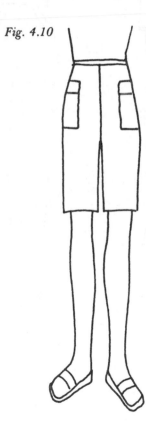

When altering pants into shorts, select slacks that fit tightly in the hips. In fact, jeans or other pants that are a little too tight for comfort are the best candidates for recycled shorts.

After you cut them to the desired length, you may find you still have to take in the sideseams.

Short shorts will be more becoming if the hemline is slanted up at the thigh, as in Figure 4.13.

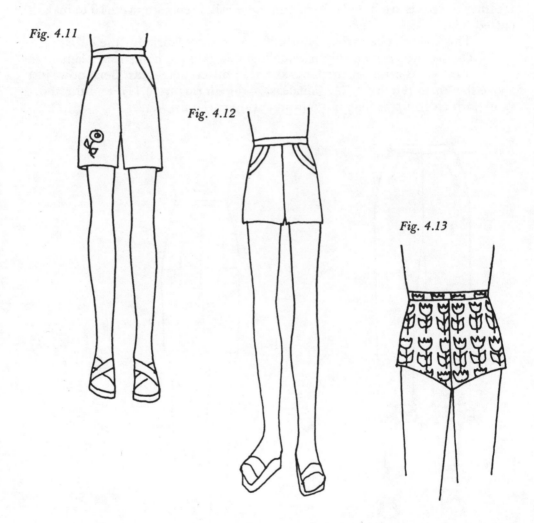

Fig. 4.11

Fig. 4.12

Fig. 4.13

KNICKERS AND CULOTTES

Knickers can be made from pants that are not too tight; there has to be enough ease on the upper leg and knee so that the legs can be gathered below the knee.

Measure to the point below the knee where you want the knickers to fit. Allow 1 inch extra for a seam and slight blousing. Cut off the pants legs when you have this measurement. Shirr the new bottoms all around the hem to fit snugly below the knees.

Open the sideseams 1 inch up from the bottom. Hem these little side openings. You will need them to get your legs through easily.

Now attach a band made of doubled fabric around the shirring at the bottom of the legs allowing two loose ends long enough to tie at the side openings in the seams. These bands can also be made shorter and finished with a button and buttonhole instead of ties.

Fig. 4.14   *Fig. 4.15*

Fig. 4.16

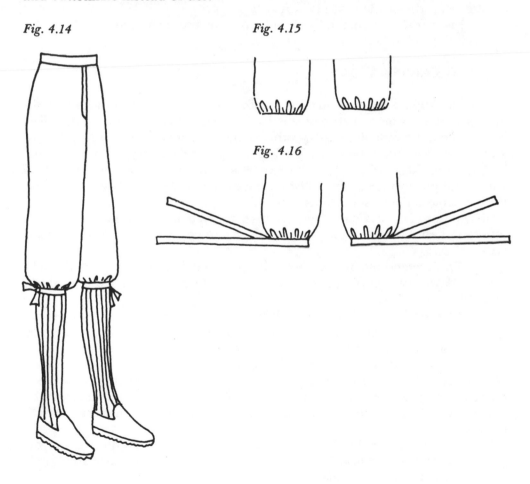

Fig. 4.17

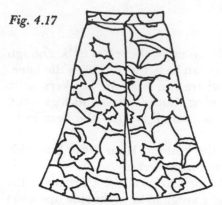

Culottes or gauchos require wide-legged pants, the wider the better. If you have any patio or palazzo pants with wide flared legs, converting them into culottes with the divided skirt look is very simple.

Just cut the legs off to the length you like and hem them.

MAKING PANTS LARGER

When pants get a bit too snug for comfort, they can be made wider by the insertion of a ribbon or a strip of suitable fabric into the sideseams as described in the section on widening skirts. If this method is not sufficient or appropriate and you are desperate about saving a favorite pair of slacks, try inserting triangular pieces of fabric with a ¼-inch seam. Place one triangle in the center back seam, fitting the wide part into the belt and the tapered point toward the crotch. Do the same on both side fronts; you will have to slash where the front darts usually occur. The fabric for these triangles might come from the hems (substitute false hems) or the inside pockets (which can be replaced with lining material).

This method might work best with pants made of fabric which is a solid color or has a very small pattern, so that a slight mismatching would not be noticeable.

On the other hand, if no self fabric at all is available, inserted triangles of a stretch fabric of a color that goes well with the pants fabric might be most comfortable and quite stylish.

Another method to consider if the waist and upper part of the trousers are too tight (and letting out the seams not sufficient) is to cut them down to hiphuggers. This requires a commercial hiphugger pattern and considerable sewing skill. All the seams at the top must be opened and the pattern carefully followed.

After removing the waistband and before you do any cutting, try on your pants. Sometimes a beltless waist will provide enough ease to solve your problems. The waist can be finished with a facing of lining material.

RECYCLING MEN'S PANTS FOR WOMEN

For a number of years now women's pants have been made in styles similar to men's (and, in fact, it is quite usual for women to buy their jeans in the Men's or Boys' Department). Thus a husband's or brother's discarded or outgrown pants might be suitable for other members of the family. If the original owner finds his trousers getting too small, they might still be a bit too large for the feminine figure.

   To make the pants smaller around the hips, take in the sideseams and the center back seam. When enlarging the back seam, extend it into the belt strip even though there is no seam there. A belt loop or leather belt will cover the new seam at the waist.

   When taking in the sideseams, you can solve the problem of the pockets by lapping the side front a bit over the back. Not too much, though, so as to not distort the sideseam.

   If the legs need tapering, the sideseams should be enlarged. It is best not to touch the inside leg seam or zipper seam.

Fig. 4.18   *Fig. 4.19*

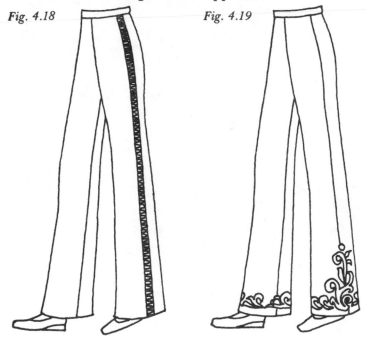

DRESSING UP TAILORED PANTS

If the occasion calls for a festive look and you can't bear to get out of your slacks, it is possible to dress up tailored pants. Most of us have seen jeans with elaborate embroidery or beading, but there are more subtle ways of dressing up legs.

One of the simplest is to stitch a black grosgrain or velvet ribbon on the side seams of black trousers. Instant tuxedo look!

The ribbon can be basted right over the sideseams all the way down and stitched close to the edge on each side of the ribbon.

If you wish to make the pants a trifle wider, you can rip the sideseams and insert the ribbon between the back and front in the same way that you would do to a skirt. Should the trousers need more width than that, it would be advisable to recycle the pants for a smaller person, or into some other garment.

For a toreador effect, try trimming the hem and the sideseams with passementerie (a commercial trimming that can be sewed on wherever you want) or novelty braid.

Another way to dress up tailored pants requires no sewing, at least for the pants. Tie a cummerbund (of roman stripes, bright-colored silk, or silky fabric) around the waist instead of a belt to transform daywear into evening attire.

5.
Coats, Jackets, and Other Outerwear

Coats and jackets are the most tailored of women's clothes; for this reason, they will generally be the most difficult for you to redesign or alter. But since they also are usually the most expensive items in the wardrobe, some effort to recycle them when styles shift will be very much worthwhile, if only to prevent an expensive garment from going to waste.

Fashions in outerwear are highly changeable. One year coats will be long, the next year short. At times, jackets or car coats will take over as the style of the moment. At other times, the raincoat is the indispensable garment. At still other times it may be vests or novelty toppers.

LENGTHENING A COAT

The most common problem is how to lengthen a coat when fashions change. Before you give up a perfectly good coat that is too short, let's see what can be done.

One way to lengthen a coat is to use a band of fur, real or fake, around the hem. This solution is feasible if you have an old fur piece that is still serviceable. An ideal fur for this conversion would be a long stole that is no longer in use.

Fake fur can be bought by the yard and, of course, costs much less than real fur. To determine how much fake fur you will need, measure around the hem of the coat. Decide how wide a band you want (adding 1 inch for seams). (Don't make the band too wide or you will have the effect of a fur skirt not a fur hem.) The band will be cut from the fur not lengthwise but selvage to selvage, so you have to know the width of the fake fur on the bolt. If it isn't wide enough to go around the hem, you will need two widths. In other words, if you want a 5 inch band (complete with seams) and one width of the fabric won't go around the hem, you will have to order 10 inches.

To make a band, cut the fur on the underside, that is, the skin side, with a razor. Care must be taken not to cut the hairs. That's the reason for using a razor and working on the wrong side so the fur or nap won't be touched.

Measure the strip to make sure it will go from one edge of the coat opening to the opposite edge.

Bind all the edges of the fur band with a strong cotton tape, ½ inch wide, on the skin, or wrong, side.

Cut a rayon lining the same size as the fur and sew it to the tape by hand. The lining should match the color of the coat.

Now, by hand, stitch on the fur strip to the bottom of the coat, from opening to opening.

Fig. 5.2

Fig. 5.1

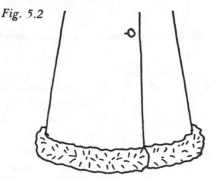

Leather, real or synthetic, can also lengthen a coat. It is easier to handle than fur and can be used with greater versatility. The leather should be of similar thickness as the wool fabric, or as close as possible.

Instead of being limited to a border at the hem, leather can be inserted in strips into several parts of the coat, depending on how much length you want to add.

In the illustrations you can see the leather inserted in the skirt part of the coat (Figure 5.3), at the midriff (Figure 5.4), and at the top, waist, and hip sections of the coat (Figure 5.5). Although the illustrations show a fitted coat, the same treatment can be used on a "tent" or loose silhouette.

It isn't necessary to alter the lining of the coat with the same type of strips.

Fig. 5.3

Fig. 5.4

Fig. 5.5

Simply add a single strip of lining fabric, in the same color or a contrast, to the hem of the existing lining to match the coat's new length.

To get the bands where you want them—and in the right width and shape—spread out the coat and place transparent tracing paper over the part where you will make the insertions.

Draw a pattern for your bands on the tracing paper. (See Figure 5.6) Small dotted lines represent the bands; the long broken lines between them indicate where you will slash the coat to insert the bands.

Cut the bands, leaving a ¾-inch seam allowance on each side of the band. The reason for such a large seam allowance is to compensate for the fabric in the coat that will be used up in the seam. Be sure to position the bands an even distance from the hem, all around the coat. When joining the band to the coat, make the seams only ⅜-inch wide.

The actual width of the band will depend on how much length you wish to add to your coat. Say the extra length you need is 4 inches, and you want it in two bands:

Allow for each band 2 inches of width plus a ¾-inch seam allowance on each side. That means you will cut each band 3½ inches wide. With ⅜-inch seams joining the bands to the coat, the bands actually will end up 2¾ inches wide (3½ minus ¾). However, you will have lost ¾ inch of coat material inserting each band. Thus each band will add 2 inches of length.

The same applies to any length you wish to add. Always add ¾-inch seam allowance to top and bottom of the band and never take in more than ⅜-inch in each seam—plus the number of inches of additional length needed for the coat, of course.

If this explanation seems very detailed, it's because I don't want you to make all this effort and then find your coat too short!

Fig. 5.6

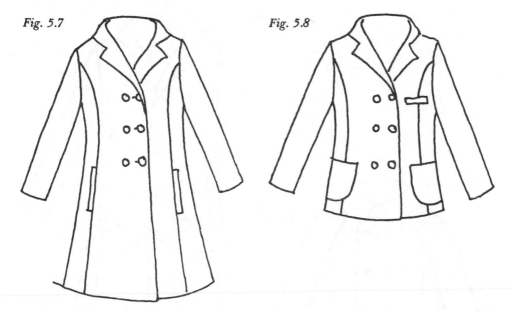

Fig. 5.7   Fig. 5.8

SHORTENING A COAT

Now we come to the coat that needs shortening to be stylish. If this is one that barely covered minidresses, consider turning it into a pants jacket. Before you snip off the hem, take a look at the style of the coat and see if there are other changes that will update it.

In Figure 5.7 you have the conventional double-breasted reefer. Figure 5.8 shows how it can be converted into a blazer type jacket.

When shortening a garment allow 2 inches for a new hem. The fabric that is cut away from the hem will be sufficient to make patch pockets.

Before sewing on the new pockets, remove the old ones from the sideseams, take off the flaps, and sew up the side openings. One of the flaps can serve as a fake breast pocket after you have cut it a bit smaller.

If you have a similar coat that is single-breasted, you can make an additional alteration by rounding the fronts. The changes are indicated by dotted lines in Figure 5.9. The bottom of the patch pockets should be rounded to correspond with the front closing.

You might also check out any sports coat, such as a tweed or camel, that may be the wrong length or need refurbishing for some other reason. These coats are often cut with raglan sleeves and can be shortened into jackets good for casual wear.

About the only alteration that was needed for the jacket in Figures 5.10-11 was cutting the coat to hip length. If there is a slit in the back of the coat, it should be opened up halfway between the waistline and hemline of the finished jacket.

Fig. 5.9

Fig. 5.10 Front

Fig. 5.11 Back

Fig. 5.12   *Fig. 5.13*

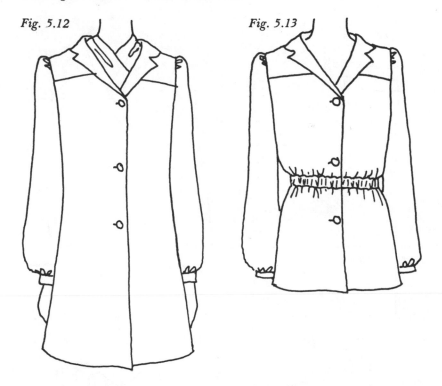

If the coat you wish to recycle into a jacket is more of a shirt cut, here are some ways of creating a different look in addition to shortening it.

Figure 5.12 is a coat with a yoke. In Figure 5.13 it is shortened into a jacket and given an elasticized waistline.

To do this sew a casing on the inside part of the coat and insert an elastic which measures the same as your waist. This will create a shirred look. The lining can be left without altering, if it is soft enough not to bulge.

The tunnel for the elastic can also be made by sewing the lining to the coat in two rows, at the waistline. The tunnel should be a trifle wider than the elastic. The lining must be bloused for extra fullness above the waist so that it won't pull the outside fabric. To do this, first pin the lining to the coat where you are going to sew it, easing the waistline of the lining to the waistline of the coat so that it blouses slightly. After pinning both rows of the tunnel, stitch the two rows. Stop the casing or tunnel ½ inch before reaching the buttons and buttonholes in the front. Also don't make your elastic so tight that it will cause the opening to gape.

Figure 5.16 shows a coat without a yoke, converted into a blouson jacket. When cutting the coat to the desired length, cut the lining about ½ inch longer plus hem allowance. This, again, is to keep the lining from pulling the coat. Sew the coat fabric and lining together in a double row like the one made for the waist elastic. Before stitching, turn the two hems ¼ inch under, toward each other, for a clean finish.

Fig. 5.14

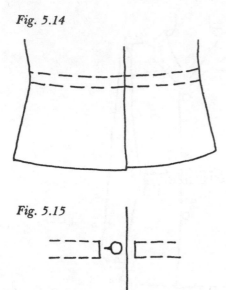

Fig. 5.16

Fig. 5.15

Fig. 5.17

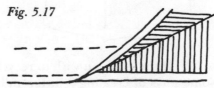

Stitch the bottom row as close to the edge as you can.

The top row should be stitched far enough above to allow a cord to be inserted. In this style I wouldn't use an elastic to thread the tunnel; a rope or cord will look more attractive. You will have to make openings at the front edges through which the rope can come out and tie. The openings can be finished by hand with an overcast stitch. These small openings must be made on the top fabric, not the lining, so that the tie or bow emerges outside, not inside the jacket.

VESTS AND TOPPERS

Coats can also be altered completely into other types of outerwear, such as vests or toppers. These can be worn over sweaters, sportwear, or dressy clothes. With sleeves removed and armholes widened, they become comfortable covers for garments that have full, flowing sleeves.

Depending on current fashions and your personal needs, toppers such as those shown in Figures 5.18 and 5.19 can be made, either sleeveless or with loose short sleeves. Sometimes a capelet replaces the sleeves.

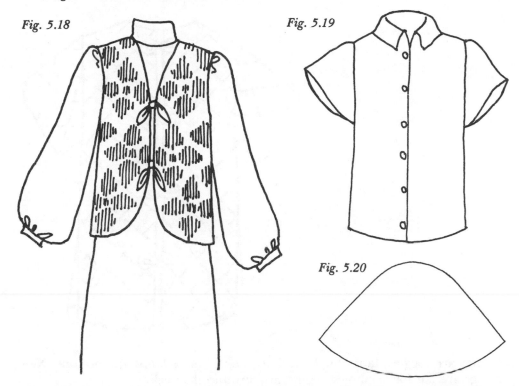

Fig. 5.18

Fig. 5.19

Fig. 5.20

When recycling a coat into a vest or short topper, it is advisable to use some garment that can't be profitably turned into a more substantial piece of apparel. Not that I wish to disparage unconventional fashion items. They are the ones that add the spark of originality and give a lift to the more routine clothes. But it is also important to have no regrets and to get the most mileage out of everything you update.

Now that you have been forewarned, let's see what will be most suitable to convert into these easy-going styles. My choice would be those coats and jackets (possibly even some dresses in heavier-weight material) that were bought on an impulse because of interesting novelty fabrics and seldom worn because they didn't coordinate with the rest of your wardrobe. In a more flippant style, they may succeed where a no-nonsense design looked out of place. Another interesting possibility is a man's vest that seldom or never gets worn with the rest of the suit. This may require only the minor alterations of making the vest tighter by taking in the sideseams, and shorter by adjusting the shoulder seams. If the vest has a back of rayon (or other lining material) instead of self fabric, it can be worn under a jacket.

Figure 5.18 shows a basic vest made from a coat or jacket from which the sleeves have been removed, armholes dropped lower, collar and front closing ripped off and cut away.

The vest meets center front and ties with novelty cords. Other suitable

Fig. 5.21

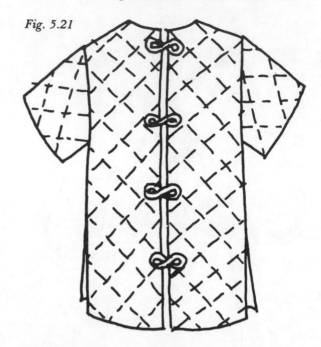

closings are toggles, fancy hooks and eyes, or Chinese loops and buttons. New facings are cut for armholes, fronts, and around ths neck.

If the coat or jacket used for this style was made of tapestry-like material, the vest can add zest to sweaters and slacks. It will also look chic over evening wear.

Figure 5.19 substitutes capelets for sleeves. But first, the armholes are dropped on this garment. Remember, you are making toppers that will slide smoothly over wide sleeves. The capelets can be made of the fabric cut away from the bottom of the coat and lined with a lining material right to the edges. The underarm seams on the capelets need not be sewn together, but left open to swing like little capes over the arm (Figure 5.20).

The hemline of the jacket can be curved at the sides if desired.

For this garment a softer fabric is best—one that has a good drape so that the capelets won't stick out like wings. A coat of velour, velveteen, or mohair would be ideal.

Figure 5.21 is a Chinese-style jacket with frog closings. This can be made from a silk or rayon evening coat, or an old cashmere coat that is beyond salvage for its original purpose.

When looking at these sketches you will notice that seams in the body aren't indicated, although they are almost certainly present in your coats. Let the seams remain where they are; they will not interfere with your new style. For example, a Chinese jacket made from the coat in Figure 5.22 will actually look like Figure 5.23 after change.

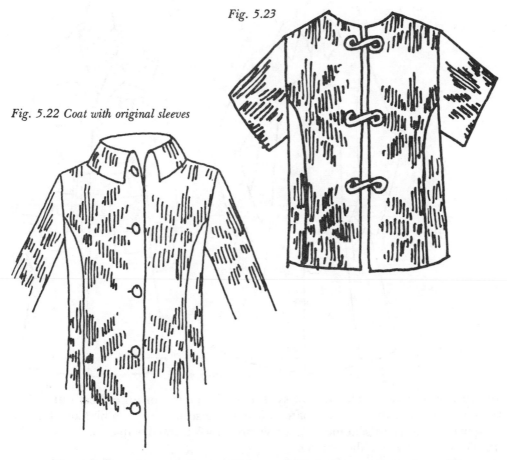

Fig. 5.23

Fig. 5.22 Coat with original sleeves

To redesign the coat into a Chinese style jacket, remove the collar and scoop out the neckline. Rip off the sleeves and cut new wide short ones from the bottom of the coat. Drop the armholes lower to accommodate the new sleeves.

Cut away the front edges with the buttons and buttonholes. Face out the new edges and neckline.

Ready-made frogs are sewn on to form new closings.

The sideseams are opened at the bottom for side slits. If the original coat has no sideseams, make the slits in the two side front seams.

RECYCLING RAINCOATS

If you look through your possessions, you may find a wearable raincoat that hasn't been used much because it is too lightweight for winter days. If that's the time of year when you get most of the damp weather, consider turning this garment into a stormcoat by adding a warm lining. This lining can be found in

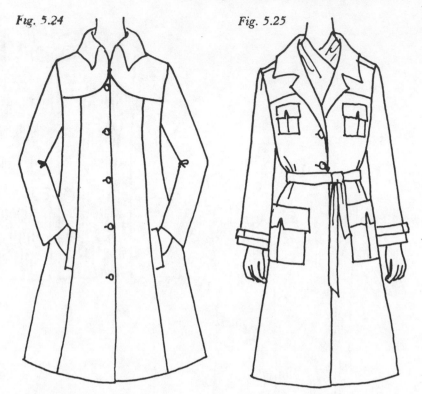

Fig. 5.24   *Fig. 5.25*

an old fur coat, or an old robe of synthetic pile fabric, or an old zip-out lining from a no-longer-used man's coat. You might also use a warm blanket that no longer fits your color scheme or is too worn to look attractive in a room but is still usable where it won't show much.

Whether the style of your raincoat is a flared shape (as in Figure 5.24) or a trench (Figure 5.25), the new warm lining is cut much the same for both. (See Figure 5.26.)

Only the body of the lining is to be cut in fur or other warm material. The sleeves should be lined in a weatherproof fabric (such as Milium, a trade name for an excellent winter lining); otherwise they will be too bulky to be comfortable. Use a commercial sleeve pattern that approximates the coat sleeve you wish to line when cutting the sleeve lining.

Cut the lining straight from the shoulders. In front, the lining should reach to the front facing with enough allowance for a seam.

Stitch the sleeve linings into the coat lining before sewing it into the coat.

Stitch the lining to the coat only (1) around the neck, (2) down the front facings, and (3) at the bottom of the sleeves. Leave the hems separate.

Chain-stitch a 1-inch string to each sideseam at the hemline of the coat and the lining, joining them at the hem. This will keep the lining from sliding around.

Fig. 5.26 (Lining body)

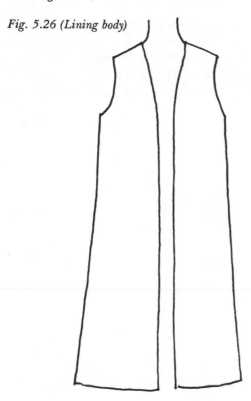

Raincoats can be lengthened with leather inserts just as can wool coats. The only difference is that the "leather" must be plastic to be waterproof and spotproof.

RECYCLING MEN'S JACKETS AND BLAZERS

Men's jackets and blazers can be converted into handsome jackets for women if there isn't a too-great disparity in size. What makes men's wear so attractive is the hard tailoring around the collar and lapels. If this part fits you without altering—and possibly destroying the fine tailoring—the rest of the jacket can be narrowed down to fit. All the recutting will take place at the sideseams, armholes, and the part of the shoulders adjoining the armholes.

Raise armholes by taking a larger shoulder seam at the sleeve end, tapered to nothing at the neck. The armhole will also become smaller when the sideseam is made larger and brought closer to the body.

To do this, rip the sideseams and the sleeves and then use a commercial pattern. The pattern will help you get your size and correct fit by showing how much to cut away. The pattern can also be used to alter the armholes and shoulders if needed.

Coats and raincoats can be treated in the same manner, if the neck, collar, and front opening can remain the same. Where this method cannot be used, these unused clothes can be considered as an additional source of fabric.

If none of these suggestions works for the coat or jacket you would like to alter, consider making it into a child's coat. You will find ideas for this conversion in Chapter 8, Children's Clothes.

6.
Remodeling Dresses

The dress has always been considered the basic unit in a woman's wardrobe. Although occasionally it is eclipsed by some other garment, it never disappears. In addition, with its many variations—from casual shirtdress to formal ballgown—a dress can be worn to any event the wearer chooses to attend.

As with other clothes, there are periodic fashion changes that require updating your dresses. The two major changes that occur in dresses, making them look new or obsolete, are in the length of the skirt and the fit of the garment. What is meant here by the fit is whether the dress falls loosely from the shoulders (Figure 6.1) or is close to the body, at least to the waist or below (Figure 6.2). As for the length, we have seen the hem travel from the ankle to the thigh and back down again.

REMODELING LOOSELY FITTED DRESSES

The loose silhouette is easier to remodel, and more versatile for conversion purposes, so let's begin there.

If you have a dress that falls loosely as in a shift (Figure 6.3), a tent (Figure 6.4), or a smock (Figure 6.5), and you want to turn it into one with a closer fit, a

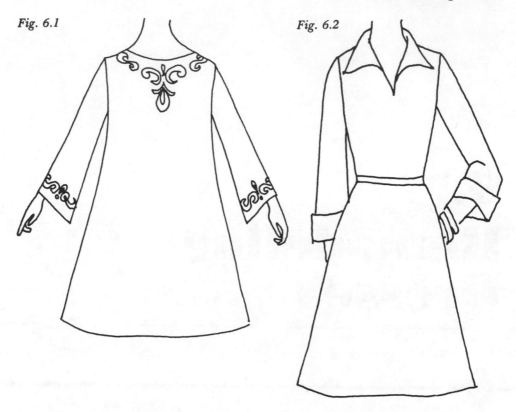

Fig. 6.1

Fig. 6.2

simple method is to make a casing at the waistline, on the underside of the dress, and run an elastic through it. There is nothing to keep you from putting the casing on the outside, if you have a decorative piece of fabric that will add an attractive touch. The result will be an interesting shirred beltline.

Figure 6.6 shows a shift with a gathered waistline, the casing used on the inside.

When a dress is cut as straight as a shift, it is sometimes advisable to make side slits by opening up the sideseams a few inches from the hemline. This gives a more graceful swing to the skirt.

If you are altering a bias-cut tent dress, instead of using an elastic at the waist try a rope belt threaded through a tunnel. To do this, make a casing at the waist, on the underside. Open the center front seam over the casing and pull through a rope or tie, knotting it in front of the dress, as in Figure 6.7.

For the dress that gets its straight lines from a smock cut, I wouldn't use any sewing to bring it closer to the body. A long sash wrapped around the waist (Figure 6.8) is more appropriate for this style.

If the three dress styles discussed above need lengthening as well, you can insert into the waistline a midriff of a contrasting fabric that goes well with the

Fig. 6.3

Fig. 6.4

Fig. 6.5

Fig. 6.6

Fig. 6.7

Fig. 6.8

Fig. 6.9

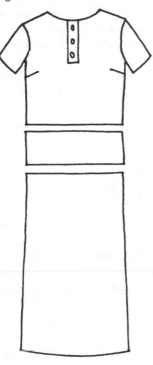

main body of the dress. Make it as wide as you require for the extra length, plus ½-inch seam allowance top and bottom.

For the shift and the smock the method is the same:

Find and mark your waistline.

Now find the center of your midriff and mark that with pins or tailor's chalk.

Measure the distance from the center to the top of the midriff. When you have this measurement, take the dress and measure the same distance from the waist up towards the bust.

Mark this line around the dress. This is where you will cut the dress to insert the midriff. That way, the middle of the midriff will be the new waistline. The seams joining the insert to the dress should be only ¼-inch wide to compensate for the absence of seam allowance on the dress.

Insert the midriff, which should be as large around as the body of the dress; in other words, it will fit into the dress without shirring or tucks.

After stitching the midriff to the top and skirt of the dress proceed with the casing and elastic as previously suggested, except that now you will put it around the center of the midriff section.

The same instructions apply to the tent dress. The one difference is finding the waistline. This type of dress is biased, so there isn't a straight line around the dress to follow easily. To overcome this difficulty, put the dress on yourself or a figure dummy. Tie a string around the waist. Pull the skirt down so that the hem is even, that is, the same distance from the floor all around. Now mark the waist with pins or tailor's chalk including the parts hidden by the folds.

Now follow the instructions for the shift.

None of the three examples used here requires a zipper if the neckline is large enough for the head to go through. Otherwise use a back neck zipper.

WIDENING THE FITTED DRESS

A fitted dress will not lend itself readily to being recycled into a chemise because of all the darts, the fitted, seamed waist, and the snug fit of the hips. It can be widened, however, if it becomes too tight for comfort.

Figure 6.10 has an insert of tucked fabric in center front, running from neck to hem. This requires splitting the center front and putting in the tucked panel—which need not be of the same fabric. A pleasing contrast in color or a sheer material that goes well with the rest of the dress will serve this purpose.

The insert should have a seam allowance on each side and a hem allowance top and bottom.

The only other work in this example is sewing in a new facing around the neck.

Increasing the width in this fashion is possible only if you need no more than 2 inches over the bust and stomach. If greater width is required, the insertions have to be distributed over several areas so as not to distort the overall fit and look of the dress.

Fig. 6.10

Fig. 6.11 Front   *Fig. 6.12 Back*

Figures 6.11-12 show an insertion on each side front and also on each side back.

This remodeling requires ripping the center of each shoulder seam. Then the dress has to be cut from shoulder to hem exactly where you want to insert the strips of fabric. These can be ribbons of commercial trim, or any patterned material that looks good on the dress. (Remember to choose materials with cleaning compatibility.)

THE TOO-SHORT FITTED DRESS

Another problem area with a fitted dress is the length. To salvage a fitted dress that is too short, you have to concentrate on the skirt.

Presuming the top fits properly, the skirt can be lengthened by adding ruffles or tiers. If the dress is very short, the skirt of the dress can be the top tier. Two other tiers, each of different fabric, can bring the length down to midcalf or lower.

The dress can stay all the same color, only the fabric pattern of the tiers being different. A more formal look can be achieved if the fabric is the same and only the color is changed. This is good for silky knits that come in many beautiful colors.

Fig. 6.13

Fig. 6.14

Fig. 6.15

The knit tiers can be joined without shirring. On the other hand, a fabric like taffeta looks pretty and bouffant when first shirred and then joined.

In Figure 6.13 the original dress was of navy and white plaid. The added middle tier is navy and white batik, the bottom tier navy and white stripe. A solid tricolor, such as red, white, and blue, could also be very attractive.

Another way of lengthening a dress is by discarding the original top and dropping the skirt to the hips. This is possible if the skirt has some shirring or soft pleats at the waist that can provide enough fullness to fit the hips.

Figure 6.14 shows a fitted waistline dress with some fullness in the skirt. Figure 6.15 shows the altered dress with a new top—a striped T-shirt. The skirt was dropped to the hips and adjusted to fit. A tie belt was sewn around the hips. A blouse can also be used in this restyling instead of a T-shirt.

If you have a short dress that you love and none of the above ideas can make it current fashion, consider it as a possible tunic to be worn over a longer skirt or a pair of pants.

Fig. 6.16

Fig. 6.17

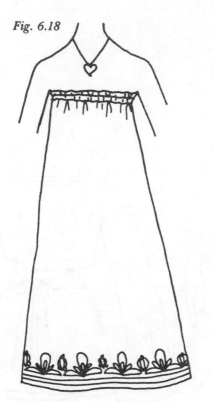

Fig. 6.18

Fig. 6.19

RECYCLING SKIRTS INTO DRESSES

A floor-length skirt can easily be made into a suntop dress for summer wear.

The method requiring the least sewing effort is to remove the waistband and sew an elastic around the top. This can be pulled up under your arms for a strapless smock or tent silhouette as in Figure 6.18

If you consider this too bare for your purpose, or prefer greater detail, a yoke and shoulder straps can be added, as in Figure 6.19.

Figure 6.18 used a shirred skirt; for Figure 6.19 the skirt was a bias-cut flare.

You can design your own yoke by using the necklines of commercial dress, blouse, or nightgown patterns that you may have around the house.

If you like a defined bustline in your sundresses, Figure 6.20 illustrates a style that can be worn for evening as well as daytime occasions.

To make this dress from a long skirt, raise the skirt to just below the bust and fit with shirrings or darts.

Make a bra top with straps (use a commercial bathing suit, sundress, or evening dress pattern) leaving the center front open. If the skirt doesn't have enough material for the bra top, use a becoming contrast or print.

Fig. 6.20

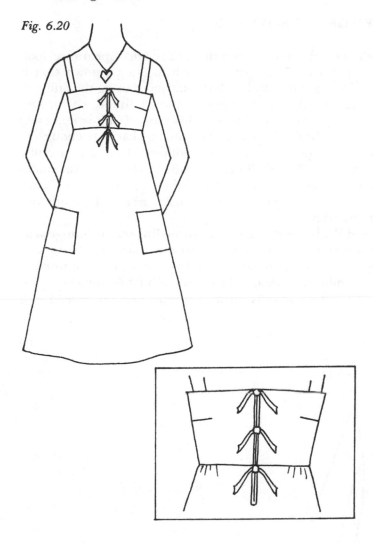

Slash an opening in the center front of the skirt to correspond with the top. This slash can be about 3 inches long. Join the top of the skirt. Finish the center opening with piping.

Make ties out of the piping, to tie the opening at the three places shown in Figure 6.20. You need six of these ties, three for each side. Sew one pair of ties into the piping at the top of the slash, another pair ties at the waistline seam, and the third pair at the halfway point between those already in place. This eliminates the zipper as well as adding interest to the dress.

If your long skirt is made of wool or some other heavy material, instead of a sundress it can be turned into a jumper to be worn over a sweater or blouse.

RECYCLING RETIRED OR UNUSED FINERY

For special occasions, when the dress can have a more dramatic appearance, look through your old evening finery. You may not wish to alter a gown that is associated with a memorable night in your life, but what about using the lining in the gown? Recently going through my souvenir clothes, I found a wrap, no longer usable, that had an exquisite silk lining. This type of silk is currently prohibitive in cost and hard to find. (If your clothes don't go back far enough to include silk linings, you might look through your mother's closets.) I carefully removed the lining, sleeves and all, and all that remained to be done was stitching up the center front openings and facing the neckline. The result, as Figure 6.21 shows, was a caftan style dress. The fabric and color were sufficiently impressive not to require any trim.

You might find hidden in some drawer elaborate lingerie or loungewear which you received as a gift and never wore because of incompatibility with scrambling breakfast eggs or dusting furniture. Nightgowns have been worn as evening dresses, and a ceremonial kimono will have enough fabric for a bouffant skirt and bolero if the current trend calls for a European peasant instead of a Japanese geisha.

Fig. 6.21

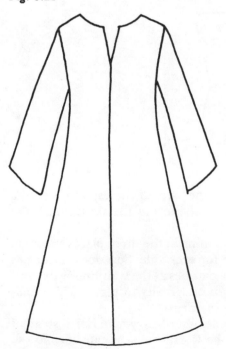

7.
Leisurewear-
A Place
for Imagination

Of all our clothes, the ones we wear during leisure hours allow the freest use of imagination. They can also be the most fun to wear—especially if they cost little or nothing to make.

Whether it is something to wear at home in your role as hostess, or outdoors just sitting around, your wardrobe and linen closet are likely to turn up suitable recycling material.

The recycled garments should be both comfortable and flattering: an apron, jumpsuit, romper suit, caftan, or other novelty clothes.

OUT-OF-THE-ORDINARY APRONS

The simplest leisure garment to make—and one that can be very stylish—is the apron. Yes, this humble garment can be very decorative and not spend all its life in the kitchen.

You have a choice of many versions. Also, any fabric that can go into the washing machine and requires little or no ironing has the right qualities.

For aprons, start by looking over the pillowcases that you rarely or never use. Many of them have ruffled or trimmed edges that can be utilized. Also look

Fig. 7.1

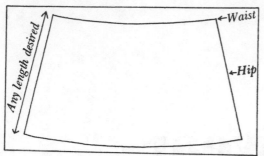

Fig. 7.2

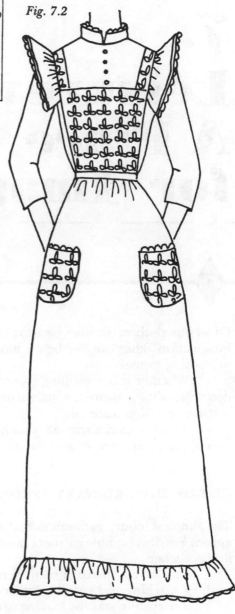

at the smaller tablecloths, especially if they are either boldly checked or delicately embroidered. A cotton skirt or dress that is out of style can also provide enough cloth for some aprons.

You may think of an apron only as something to cover your skirt while cooking. Try looking at it with a fresher and more fashion-minded view. Consider, for example, two aprons worn back and front that will cover you without the need for a skirt underneath. They can be sufficiently attractive to meet guests in.

The trick here is to make sure the aprons are wide enough to overlap one another. The overlaps on each side should be generous enough not to show anything you don't want shown. Conversely, if you're planning to wear pants or shorts under the aprons, the overlap can be skimpier to allow glimpses of the rest of your costume.

I suggest that you make two separate aprons that will be worn together, you make one with a waistband that closes with hooks and eyes instead of long ties. The waistband of the second apron can then be wrapped and tied over the first one without bulk.

To make aprons big enough to overlap at the sides is not difficult. A few simple measurements will give you the needed widths and length.

Here is how to make the two aprons:

In Figure 7.1 the waist measure on each apron is one and one-half times to twice your waist size. This is to allow enough fabric for shirring. The hip measure should be one and one-half to two times your hip measurement.

Make the aprons any length desired.

Cut two waistbands. One will fit your waistline and close with hooks and eyes. The other band should be about two and a half times your waist measurement to provide for wrapping and tying around your waist. A comfortable width for the waistband is about 1½ inches finished, but you can vary this at your discretion.

Shirr in the top of each apron so that it fits your waist, either front or back, from side to side, with a few extra inches for the overlaps at each side.

Attach the waistbands to the aprons. The hems and sides can be hemmed or finished off with ruffles. Either apron can be worn separately, of course.

An apron can be converted into a pinafore by adding a bib and shoulder straps.

The bib and straps need not be of matching fabric. An attractive print that goes well with the apron can be used for these small pieces.

Ruffles and pockets can also be added if you want a traditional look.

There is no need to be traditional, however. There are modern pinafores, really coverall aprons, that wrap around you. They usually can be worn by themselves as well as over other clothes.

Your starting point here would be an old back-wrap skirt that you'd like to recycle.

Fig. 7.3 Front   *Fig. 7.4 Back*

Figures 7.3-4 show how the skirt converts into a coverall apron by the attaching of a top and straps.

By extending the bib to cover the sides and a little of the back, you can dispense with a shirt or blouse underneath.

Another good top for these wraparound aprons is the halter neckline (Figures 7.5-6).

Here you cut the halter (Figure 7.7) to extend from one end of the back-wrap skirt to the other.

Join the top and skirt at the waist.

Sew casing at the neckline; through this goes a drawstring. This is pulled to fit and then tied around the neck. The whole garment is wrapped together by the belt on the skirt.

An embroidered tablecloth or any unused household linens that have the edges finished in scallops or with lace can make an apron-pinafore with two

Fig. 7.5 Front

Fig. 7.6 Back

Fig. 7.7

Fig. 7.8

well-cut panels, one panel making the front, another panel for the back, and some ties at shoulders and sides (or loops and buttons if you prefer). If you're converting something that has no embroidery or finished edges, you can make your own scallops, lining them with a bright print or edging them with a contrasting piping. Figure 7.8 shows how this works.

There are no shoulder seams or sideseams. The panels are the same back and front. This can be worn over a jumpsuit or a long T-shirt.

JUMPSUITS

And that brings us to another comfortable leisure garment: the jumpsuit. This also lends itself well to imaginative styling. A jumpsuit can be ankle-length, a romper, or anything in between.

The basis for a jumpsuit is a pair of pants. The easiest to work with are the pull-ons with elasticized waists. For the top part, blouses, shirts, and T-shirts are all suitable. For use in a jumpsuit, fabrics with a stretch (such as knits) are more comfortable.

If you are going to make a strapless or halter top jumpsuit, leftover remnants from other recycled clothes may have a sufficient amount of fabric for the top. My favorite style, for any kind of garment, is the one that requires no zippers or other closures.

This brings us again to the elastic or drawstring.

Figure 7.9 shows a jumpsuit that has an elasticized waistline. Another elastic around the top keeps the whole thing in place.

To make this suit, start with a pair of pants with an elasticized waist, the pull-on kind. Remove the elastic and the casing, if any, because first you will have to join the top to the pants at the waist.

The pants should look like Figure 7.10 before you join the top.

The pattern for the top is shown in Figure 7.11. As you can see, it is simply an oblong piece of cloth measuring the same at top and waist.

Between its top and bottom, the measurement should be whatever you measure from under your arm to your waist. Allow 2 inches for the waist seam and a bend-back at the top to make a casing for the elastic.

The width of the fabric for the top should be the same as the circumference of the pants waistline after the elastic has been removed.

There need be only one seam in the top (aside from the waistseam) in the center back joining the two ends.

After joining the top and pants, put a casing around the waistline. Also bend back the top to form another casing or tunnel, as illustrated in Figure 7.13.

Cut two lengths of elastic, one to fit your waist and one to go around you under your arms and above the breasts. A comfortable width for the elastic would be about ½ inch.

Insert these elastics into the appropriate casings. Done!

For jumpsuits with fitted waistlines, you need pants with zippers in front or back, depending on the style.

Figure 7.14 shows a front-zippered jumpsuit which combines fitted slacks with a cut-off blouse. The right blouse for this style would have a front opening, probably buttoned.

Since the jumpsuit is easier to make and wear if it has a single zipper to close the pants and top, the blouse's center front strips containing the buttons and buttonholes are cut away, down from the collar to the hem of the blouse (Figure 7.15).

The cut front edges of the blouse are faced out with attractive material. (Later the zipper will be placed in here.)

Next the blouse has to be shortened. The correct length is your measurement from back neck to back waist, plus ½ inch for seam and 1 inch for ease at the back when you sit or move around. This 1½ inch allowance at the center back should be tapered to ¾ inch at center front.

Now the blouse has to be fitted with darts or shirring, back and front, to measure the same as the pants around the waist.

Now you are ready to prepare the pants:

Fig. 7.9

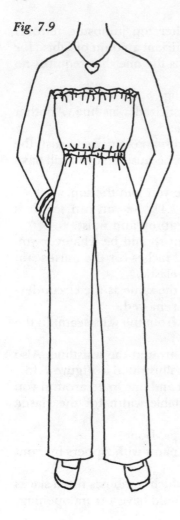

Fig. 7.10

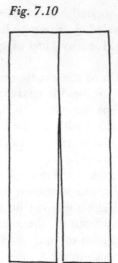

Fig. 7.11 Top waist

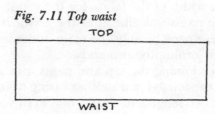

TOP

WAIST

Fig. 7.12 Back   *Fig. 7.13*

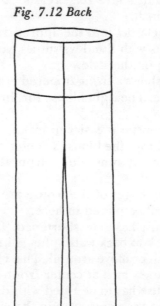   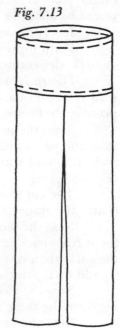

Fig. 7.14

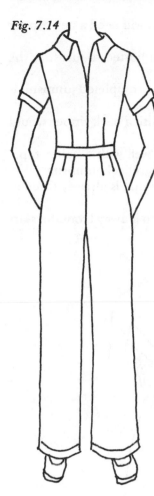

Fig. 7.15

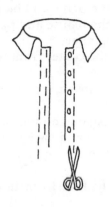

Fig. 7.16

Fig. 7.17

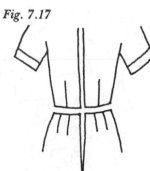

Fig. 7.18

Fig. 7.19

Remove the waistband, if any, and the zipper. You will need a new zipper that is long enough to zip up the pants and blouse.

When the waistlines of the blouse and pants are adjusted to measure the same, sew the two waistlines together.

Put the new zipper into the center front seam. The completed jumpsuit is seen in Figure 7.19.

For a bareback, dressy jumpsuit, a pair of pants with a back zipper would be ideal.

A soft, flowing palazzo pajama bottom would go well with a halter top.

Figures 7.20-21 show front and back views of a bareback jumpsuit.

The top can be made from the top of a minidress that is already fitted at the waist and has a back zipper.

To prepare the top for the transformation, first rip it away from the skirt of the dress.

Fig. 7.20 Front   *Fig. 7.21 Back*

Remove the zipper and put it aside for later use.

Cut the neckline to whatever halter style best suits you, using a commercial pattern or your own design; always remember to leave seam allowances when you are your own designer.

Fit the waistline with darts or shirring, so that it measures the same as the waistline of the pants. Finish the neckline completely, with ties and ruffles; or if you like, use the tie only around the neck, leaving the rest plain.

Remove the waistband (if there is one) from the pants.

Remove the pants zipper. You will use the longer one from the dress.

Join the top and bottom at the waistline.

Insert the dress zipper into the center back seam. If it is too long, you might be able to shorten it; most zippers can be cut off at the bottom and the ends closed by stitching through by hand around the cut edges.

COVERALLS AND ROMPER SUITS

Jumpsuits need not be ankle-length. The legs can be cut to whatever length you find most becoming.

Figure 7.22 shows a short coverall. This is nothing more than a pair of shorts, back-zippered, with a bib and suspenders added. The bib can be made of any scrap of fabric that combines well with the fabric of the shorts. For the suspenders, you might try using a commercial webbing or braid, or a sturdy wide trim.

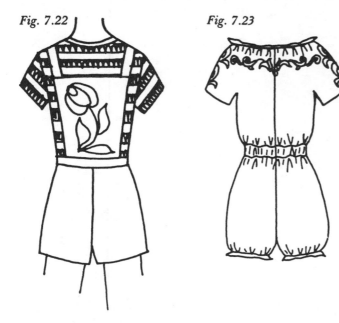

Fig. 7.22   *Fig. 7.23*

Figure 7.23 shows a shirred romper suit. The elasticized (or drawstring) neck and waist make it possible to dispense with the zipper.

A peasant-type shirt or blouse with enough length through the body will have sufficient material to be converted into a romper.

You will need a commerical pattern to get the shape of the panty bottom. Try using a pattern for a bathing suit bottom to get the right fit, provided the shirt or blouse that you are recycling doesn't have a center seam. You can cut the legs a bit longer and fuller to allow for shirring in the hems.

CAFTANS

Caftans are also easy to make and comfortable to wear, and enjoy periodic popularity. Essentially, a caftan is simply a form of long poncho with defined shape for arms.

Striped or flowered sheets, draperies or curtains that are no longer used (as long as they are not made of glass fiber), embroidered linens that are consigned to the back of the closet, are all suitable for this style. Printed bed throws that no longer fit in with your color scheme can also be recycled into caftans.

If there isn't enough fabric—for example, say you are planning to use a fairly small tablecloth, or a retired long skirt—make a short caftan to wear with pants in a harmonizing color.

Caftans can be very simple—merely graceful folds of fabric—or elaborately decorated.

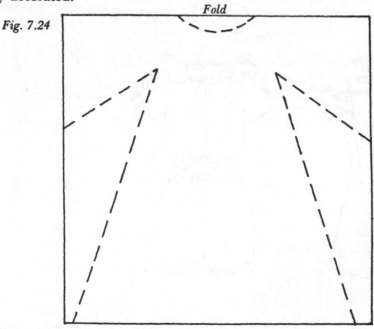

Fold

Fig. 7.24

Although commercial patterns show a variety of styles for caftans, Figure 7.24 provides a basic pattern that can be altered to suit individual tastes.

The fabric is folded over in the center, making the back and front identical. The fabric can be pieced with a seam at the fold if it isn't long enough to fold in half. Or you can use different materials, seamed at the fold, provided they make a pleasing combination.

The dotted lines in the illustration form a pattern of an unfitted garment that slips over the head. The sleeves need not be that clearly defined. The only stitched seam (other than in the fold) is from under the arm to about the knee in an A-line. Baste it first to make sure you can slip it easily over the head.

Figure 7.25 shows only partial sideseams; the rest of the fabric on each side will automatically drape over the arms. Aside from the neckline the fabric is not cut.

Here, an oval embroidered table cloth was folded over. At the top, the neckline was cut out and slashed at front to allow it to slide over the head.

Necklines on these garments can be round, V-shaped, or squared, if you prefer these to the slashed version. Cut the neckline a little closer to the throat than the finished line will be, to allow for the seam around the neck.

Novelty edging, embroidery, and piping are often used for decoration around neck, sleeves and hem. (See Chapters 11 and 12.)

When using sheer fabrics for caftans, a more dramatic effect can be achieved if, instead of lining the caftan, it is worn over a strapless jumpsuit.

Fig. 7.25

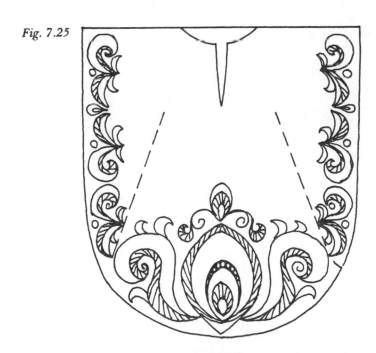

8.
Children's Clothes

Recycling clothes for children provides an opportunity to make use of the too-small, too-little-fabric items in your wardrobe.

While black crepe as of this writing has not yet come in fashion for school wear, there has been a considerable blurring of the differences between adult and children's textiles and styling, and most adult fabrics these days are readily adaptable to children's wear. In particular, the wash-and-wear varieties will be suitable for the child's play and school life. And the popularity of sportswear among children makes it possible to utilize even very small leftovers.

Perhaps the most charming of the recycled fabrics for use in children's clothing and accessories is whatever patchwork you can accumulate. If you set aside the washable odds and ends of material, you will find that even small pieces can be useful. Tiny vests, aprons, and bibs can be made from these patches. Larger patchwork can be stitched into laundry and pajama bags, wall hanging, and "organizers" with lots of pockets sewn on to them to hold the treasures children possess. There are commercial patterns for all of these ideas if you need help with them. (See Chapter 10 for how to make patchwork.)

Fig. 8.1   Fig. 8.2   Fig. 8.3

CHILDREN'S TOPS

The easiest garments to make, and to wear, are loose tops. These can be made very short to go with shorts or beach wear, or long enough to serve as dresses or to wear over slacks.

In the tops shown in Figures 8.1 and 8.2 you have a minimum of work and fabric. These tops can be made from the skirts of your old minidresses, from unusable skirts, and from blouses, as long as everything is washable. The pockets need not be of the same cloth or color. In fact, different bits of prints will look attractive as straps and the pockets.

Figure 8.3 is a top that can be made of strips of fabric only a few inches wide. Here again nothing needs matching. Combinations of calico prints in an assortment of colors or of gingham checks and stripes will make attractive groupings.

For all three tops illustrated here, you need patterns only for the neckline and the armholes. If you have a commercial pattern for a child's dress, you can easily make the necessary adjustments. Since all three tops are loose, a little extra fullness won't matter.

Fig. 8.4   *Fig. 8.5*

JUMPERS

If there is additional material, these tops can easily become jumpers. About the only changes required are more length and deeper armholes to allow room for a blouse underneath.

Figure 8.4 shows a jumper cut from a miniskirt that didn't have enough fabric for the straps to be cut from the same material. The pockets and the straps are made of printed fabric scraps.

In Figure 8.5 the skirt of the jumper is of denim, the bib is polka dot, and the pockets and straps are plaid gingham. Far from looking odd, such combinations can make these garments fresh and original.

SKIRTS AND SHORTS

If the available fabric is less than what you need for a dress or a jumper, it can be cut simply as a skirt.

Fig. 8.6

Fig. 8.7

Fig. 8.8

Fig. 8.9

Figure 8.6 is a striped cotton skirt made from an old apron. The pockets and the waistband—which can tie in a bow in the back—are made of flowered cotton remnants.

Figure 8.7 shows a tailored suspender skirt made of camel cloth that was left over when a camel coat was converted into a pants jacket.

Children's flared skirts and shorts take about the same amount of fabric. The striped seersucker pull-on shorts (Figure 8.8) were made from a short seersucker breakfast coat, using a commercial pattern for fit.

The short denim overall (Figure 8.9) was made from the leftover legs of a pair of adult jeans that were transformed into shorts. The legs were opened on the inside seams (left intact on the outside seam). The crotch was pieced to fit a commercial pattern. Pockets, straps, and belt are of calico. The back belt is elasticized to eliminate closings.

BEACHWEAR FROM TOWELING

The linen closet can contribute useful material in the form of terry cloth bath towels that may have been retired because of a change in the color scheme. These can be converted into children's beachwear, shorts, creepers, and coveralls to go over damp suits and bodies. A commercial pattern will enable you to get a correct size and fit, but you can exercise your ingenuity in the use of fabric.

Fig. 8.10

Figure 8.10 shows two different colored towels combined in a terry cloth jumpsuit. If the child's size is small enough, there may be enough material to make a matching hood to dry a wet head.

If necessary, use a commercial child's jumpsuit pattern to guide you. Make a center front and back seam even if they don't occur in the pattern.

The hood can be sewn to the neck of the jumpsuit, or tied on separately.

RECYCLING WOMEN'S SLACKS AND SHORTS FOR CHILDREN

Women's slacks that are no longer stylish can be altered to fit a child, if the fabric is suitable. I'm thinking here of printed pants that periodically make an appearance and then seem to disappear from the fashion scene. This type of fabric might look very good on an 8-or 9-year-old.

Instead of ripping the pants completely apart, try cutting them down at the outside of the leg, at the bottom, and at the waist. The dotted lines in Figure 8.11 illustrate where to cut. If there isn't a great difference in size between the adult and child, there will be no need to alter the crotch and inner leg seams.

Fig. 8.11   *Fig. 8.12*

To alter the waist you will first remove the zipper (replacing it with a shorter one after the remodeling).

There should be enough fabric for a new waistband and a patch pocket or two.

The same method can be used whether the pants are flared or straight. Be careful not to cut away the flare when you are narrowing the legs at the bottom.

Women's shorts can also be altered in this fashion to fit a child. Children's pants vary in length, as do those of adults, from ankle-length to short shorts. A woman's Bermuda or walking shorts may be long enough to be converted into a child's clamdiggers. If a little more length is needed, as shown in Figure 8.12, this can be done, by adding a bottom and cuff of a different fabric.

Here white walking shorts were taken in at waist and down the outside leg seam to fit the child. Then checked bottoms long enough to form turned-up cuffs were added. A checked pocket was stitched on for trim.

REMODELING COATS FOR CHILDREN

Children's coats and outerwear account for a large share of the family clothing budget, so any coats and jackets which you no longer wear and which can be recycled into such garments deserve special effort.

There is a great deal of difference between altering a coat for a 12-year-old and making a toddler's Sunday-best wrap. Before altering a coat or any other garment for a young teen or pre-teen, it would be a good idea to get his or her opinion on what constitutes a desirable style. This also will do much to prevent the feeling of getting a hand-me-down.

If the coat that you plan to remodel for a pre-teen is small and short to begin with, there may be no need to rip it all apart. The most likely changes will be smaller shoulders and narrower fit through the bustline. This will require ripping out the sleeves and removing the lining to make the same changes as in the coat.

The dotted line in Figure 8.13 shows where the shoulder was cut narrower. The armholes were made smaller by stitching the sideseams higher. The sideseams also were taken in on the upper body to the extent necessary to make the coat smaller. This increase in the sideseams can taper to nothing at the waist if the skirt and hemline of the coat are not too big. Otherwise, take in the sideseams all the way down.

The sleeves also will have to be taken in to fit the new armhole. This means removing a little of the "head" at the top of the sleeve and taking in a little at the underarm seam.

If, for some reason, the neckline and top aren't suitable for a child's coat, they can be cut off and a yoke of fake leather or suede or a novelty coating fabric can be styled in a new top appropriate for a young person, as shown in Figure 8.14. Use a commercial child's coat pattern for the shape of the yoke and its

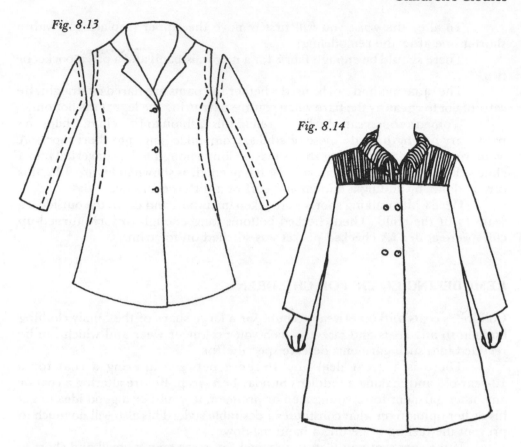

Fig. 8.13

Fig. 8.14

placement on the coat. The sleeves can either remain in the original fabric or be made of the same material as the yoke. It would be helpful to check the children's coat departments in stores, to see what the current styles in collars, pockets, and trimmings are. You can use these ideas for the recycled coat to bring it in line with popular juvenile taste.

As for making a toddler's coat from a grownup one, it would be far better to take the original coat completely apart, press out all the seams, and work with a commercial pattern the way you would with new fabric. For such a small garment it would be most economical to use an old jacket, or even the leftover bottom part of a coat that has been converted into a short topper.

RAINCOATS, RAINCAPES, AND PONCHOS

When selecting coats for recycling, don't overlook the raincoats and raincapes.

For the raincoats, the same procedure applies as for regular coats.

Raincapes, however, can become excellent ponchos, which are much

Fig. 8.16

Fig. 8.15

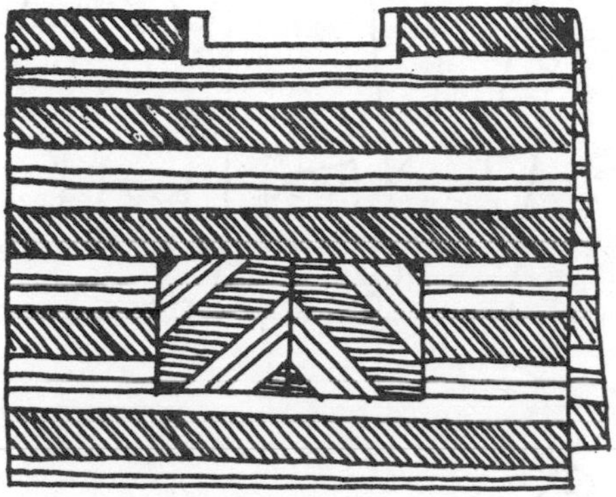

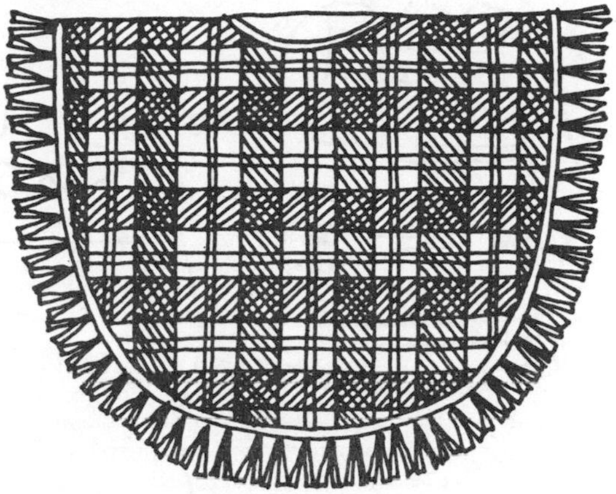

easier garments to make. Ponchos can also be made out of wool or acrylic blankets.

There are commercial patterns for ponchos, but the easiest are the oblongs or ovals folded in half. Figure 8.15 is an oblong blanket folded in half, with a shallow square neckline cut to alow the head through. The neckline is bound by novelty tape, and a divided kangaroo pocket is sewn on the front.

Figure 8.16 is another blanket, folded in half and cut to oval shape. The hem is finished with a fringed tape and the neckline bound with a matching tape without the fringe.

INFANTS' AND TODDLERS' CLOTHES

For infants' and toddlers' clothes where fabric requirements are very small, the emphasis is frequently on delicate hand embroidery. To achieve this, seldom-used cocktail napkins, guest towels, hankies, or an ethnic blouse you have tired of can provide you with instant handwork.

These small linens will make yokes, borders, sleeves, and pockets for basic garments. There are commercial patterns for simple styles that depend on the trimming to make them individual.

The most common shapes for infants and toddlers are the skimmer, the yoked dress, and the romper or crawler.

The skimmer (Figure 8.17) can be made of any crisp cotton such as gingham checks; you might use remnants from a cut-up washable tablecloth,

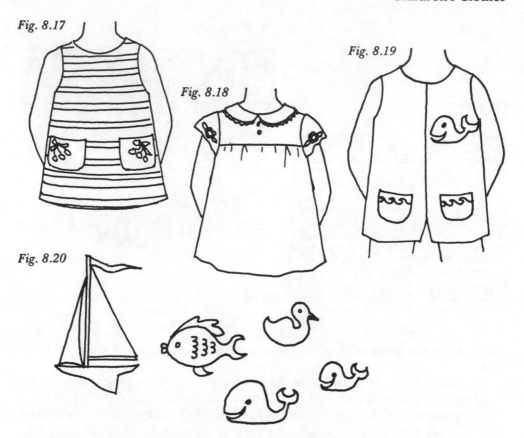

Fig. 8.17

Fig. 8.18

Fig. 8.19

Fig. 8.20

napkins, or some remodeled garments. Piqué is also a good choice if recycling of a piqué skirt left some unused fabric. An embroidered hankie can add a decorative pocket. This would also be a very good time to make use of any patchwork (see Chapter 10) you've accumulated.

Figure 8.18 illustrates a typical yoked infant dress. A lightweight batiste or other thin cotton from a daintily printed summer blouse, or a pastel pillow slip, will serve well for this purpose. The sleeves, either puffed or ruffled, are converted cocktail or luncheon napkins. The front yoke can also be of some embroidered cloth. The trick here is not to cut up a serviceable linen set but to use up a couple of odd napkins left over and still in good condition.

Figure 8.19 is a romper that can take sportier fabrics. Terry cloth towels would be very practical, but linen hand towels can also be suitable. This is particularly true of those that are embroidered with ducks or fish as the bathroom motif.

Sewing for your two- to five-year-old child can be fun. That's because the days of the undershirt and diaper are over and the time of the fashion critic has not, as yet, arrived. And the ever-present blue jeans and sneakers can still be held at bay.

Fig. 8.21

Fig. 8.22

Fig. 8.25

Fig. 8.24

Fig. 8.23

This is your opportunity to indulge in pleasing yourself when dressing your angel or imp, so make the most of it.

Since most clothes will be outgrown in a matter of months and the fabric requirements for these garments are small, the use of leftovers from recycled and other sewing projects can have an important impact in this area.

If you have any vests, either men's or women's, that are no longer worn, they can be converted into outdoor jackets and even coats if the child is small enough. The missing sleeves and neckline can be made of bright plaids or velveteen (Figure 8.21), depending on the fabric in the vest. The way to work this out is to take the vest apart, but do try to leave the buttonholes intact. They are usually small enough to be suitable for a child.

Use a commercial pattern, preferably one that has some kind of yoke or collar that is suitable for filling in the cutaway neckline of the vest. Otherwise, try a cardigan style.

Cotton petticoats, saved because they were too pretty to throw away, can be converted into dresses, pinafores and tops for the small set. Even a few ruffles can be made into an apron for an existing dress and freshen its appearance.

Simply sew together two or three rows and shirr onto a waistband.

If you are altering a full skirt into a slim one for yourself, there may be enough left over for a matching daughter skirt. This is the age when looking like mother is considered an asset, so don't pass up the opportunity. Check the illustrations for easy-to-do women's leisurewear for additional ideas.

9.
Sleeves and Other Arm Fashions

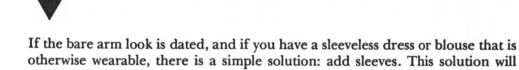

If the bare arm look is dated, and if you have a sleeveless dress or blouse that is otherwise wearable, there is a simple solution: add sleeves. This solution will work equally well for dresses or blouses that you're simply bored with or that you feel "don't do anything for you."

The current styles may not require matching fabric for the new sleeves. In fact, some form of contrast will actually give a lift to a tired garment.

Before buying any fabric, look around to see if there is something suitable already in the house. The one thing to remember, as always, is that the material in the new sleeves must be compatible for cleaning purposes with the rest of the garment.

Don't forget to check out the scarves. A pair of bandana kerchiefs can make excellent sleeves for sporty dresses or blouses. Patchwork, made of all the scraps you've been saving, will go with almost anything and can be very attractive. A white sheer fabric, such as voile or cotton lace, can solve the problem for dressier clothes. Material left over from sheer recycled curtains (provided they're not glass fiber) could work well. This is also the time to reach for the odd leftover embroidered napkins and other linens that remain from now incomplete sets. If there isn't enough material for a long sleeve, short ones or little capelets will do.

Fig. 9.1

Fig. 9.2

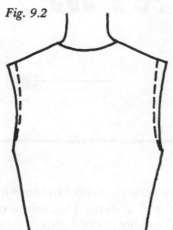

Fig. 9.3

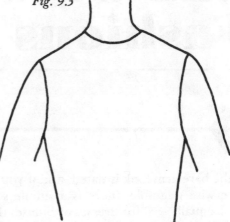

Fig. 9.4

Fig. 9.5

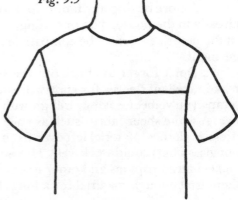

Fig. 9.6   *Fig. 9.7*

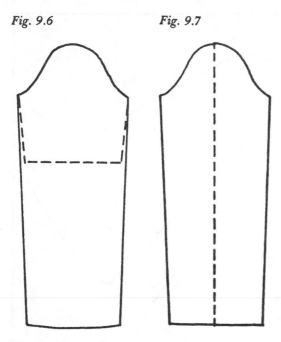

Before adding the sleeves, you must first prepare the armholes of the garment you're altering. Here is how you do it.

Rip out—very carefully—the facing or binding that you'll find around the armhole. Press out the old seam. There is no need to open the shoulder or underarm seams.

Now take a commercial pattern you have used before and check its armhole with the one you're altering. Sometimes the shoulder on a sleeveless garment extends over the arm and you may have to trim away the excess fabric, as in Figure 9.2.

Other times the armhole on the garment may be cut away too much to set in a regular sleeve (see Figure 9.3).

There are several ways to deal with this.

You can use a raglan sleeve from a commercial pattern (Figure 9.4).

Or you can cut a new yoke to go with the new sleeves (Figure 9.5). Use a commercial pattern to fit the yoke and sleeves properly. Don't forget to leave seam allowances on the yoke and body of the dress for joining.

When the original armhole is suitable for a set-in sleeve, you can proceed after deciding on the style. Study the types of sleeves at the end of this chapter; they may give you ideas to work from.

Use a commercial paper sleeve pattern that you have used and liked before, changing it in the following fashion to fit in with your ideas.

To shorten the sleeve: Cut at the desired length and taper at the seam (follow the dotted lines in Figure 9.6).

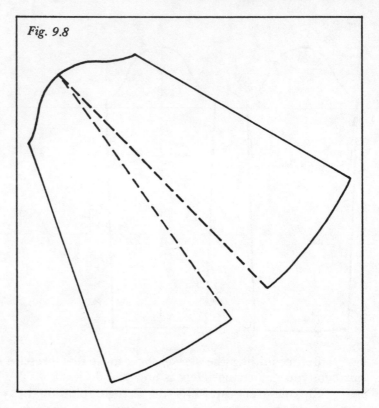

Fig. 9.8

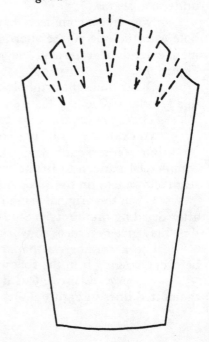

Fig. 9.9

To widen the sleeve: Split the pattern down the center (dotted line in Figure 9.7) and spread it apart until you get the width you want. You can make the sleeve as wide as you want, as long as the two sides of the pattern touch at the very top.

To make a capelet type sleeve, short or long: Place the pattern on the bias of the fabric. Split the pattern down the center, keeping the top joined, and spread the bottom to the desired width. (See Figure 9.8.) The flare of the sleeve can be increased to a half circle by spreading the pattern sufficiently.

If you want to shirr the top of the sleeve to make it puffed, but not widen the bottom, slash the top of the pattern in several places and spread as in Figure 9.9.

Fig. 9.10   *Fig. 9.11*

Fig. 9.12   *Fig. 9.13*

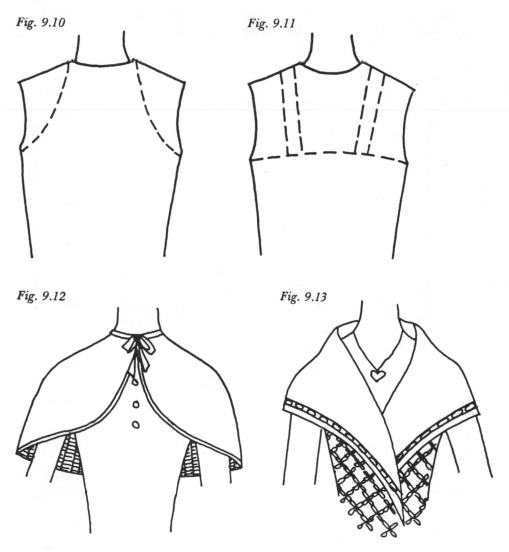

You can also revitalize sleeveless garments without adding sleeves—by cutting away the armholes even more.

For examples, Figure 9.10 converts to a halter. Mark the halter lines with basting thread, back and front. Cut the armholes away, saving the fabric for facings.

Figure 9.11 makes a suntop. Cut along the dotted line, back and front. The shoulder straps can be made of the cut-away fabric, ribbon, or contrasting material.

Instead of sleeves, capes and capelets can provide interest and cover for arms.

A dress that becomes a blouse may have enough fabric left over from the skirt to make a separate little cape (or shawl) to tie around the neck (Figure 9.12). The cape may be lined with an interesting fabric and edged with a piping.

Fig. 9.14

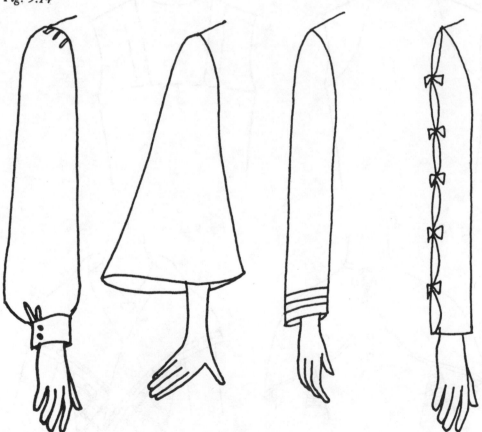

If the neckline is changed to a large collar, either sailor type or side-wrap, the arms can be partly covered without adding sleeves (Figure 9.13). There are many commercial patterns with this type of collar that can be used to guide you.

To help you with ideas, the sketches included show an assortment of sleeves that could be helpful to you in your recycling. There are commercial patterns that can be adjusted very easily to suit your needs, or use these just as inspiration for your own designs. If you are using a commercial pattern, choose the one closest to the style you would like and use it to guide you for the armhole fit and the look you want.

The illustrations show long sleeves but all of them can be made in shorter versions simply by moving the bottom part of the sleeve (which is often the decorative part) further up the arm.

Fig. 9.15

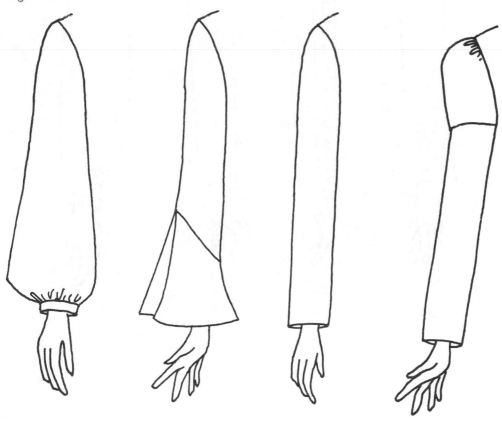

Fig. 9.16

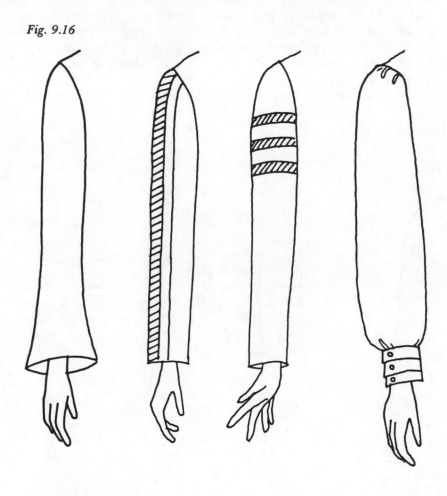

10.
Patchwork and Other Bits and Pieces

Anyone who sews will accumulate a lot of remnants too attractive to throw away, yet too small or odd-shaped for conversion into conventional garments. Save these small bits and pieces. There are many useful and decorative things you can make from them.

None, perhaps, is more useful and decorative than patchwork material which is pieced together and then converted into clothing or trim.

Those readers who are expert at patchwork might want to use the scraps for the traditional hand-sewn version. For use in clothing, however, where the fit of the garment is of primary importance, square patches of equal size joined together by machine will be much easier to cut and fit. This means shifting the design emphasis from the shape of the patches to the colorings and prints of the different fabrics.

The size of the squares will depend, to some extent, on the type of garment the patchwork is meant for. For example, a child's blouse will look better with a smaller square than one used for a woman's blouse. In any case, a square that errs on the small side generally looks more attractive.

An easy way to join the squares without having any corners to worry about is to join them first in a row. A seam allowance of ⅜ inch should be sufficient. The rows can be fairly short or quite long, depending on what you are planning to do with the patchwork.

Fig. 10.1   *Fig. 10.2*   *Fig. 10.3*

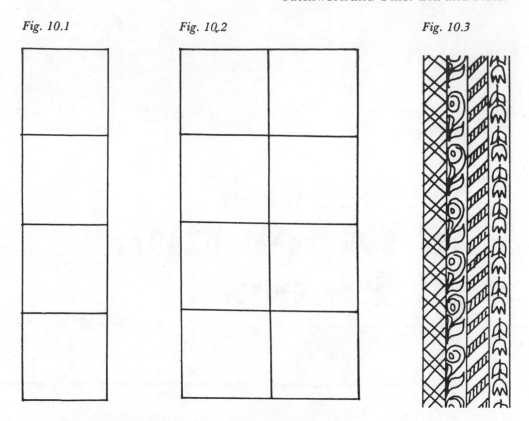

Next you join the rows, as in Figure 10.2

If you make a paper pattern of the square and cut all the fabric scraps precisely to this pattern, the squares will meet properly at corners.

Beginners need not be discouraged, however. Commercial patchwork clothes will often not be that accurate, so you don't have to be perfect!

Another interesting way of joining fabrics is in long strips, as shown in Figure 10.3. Different patterns form "ribbons' across the fabric. This method works well if your remnants consist of leftover lengths from sewing projects. Use a ⅜-inch seam to join the fabric strips. Ribbons can be joined this way, too, but the cost may be prohibitive for sufficient yardage. A less expensive alternative is to insert an occasional ribbon between the strips of fabric, preferably a ribbon you already have in your scrap bag. You may also insert strips of lace or embroidery, depending on the types of fabrics you are combining. Here, again, everything should be dry-cleanable or washable. The materials can also be grouped according to dressiness or casualness—all the washable cottons and synthetics that look like cotton in one group, and the rayons, velvets, taffetas, and such in another.

After you acquire sufficient yardage of patchwork, you can proceed with the process of turning it into new clothes.

Fig. 10.4

Fig. 10.5

Fig. 10.6

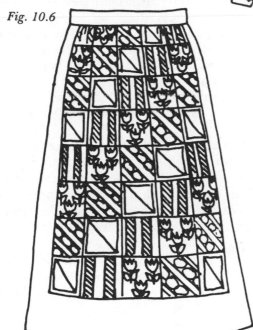

A whole dress or long skirt will require a considerable amount of patch-work cloth. If you don't have the patience or sufficient scraps for a major project, try something smaller.

A short bolero (Figure 10.4) or sleeveless vest (Figure 10.5) can go over a number of costumes; they require little yardage and can give a very striking effect. Clothes made of patchwork are best lined from edge to edge so as not to show all the seams of the joined patches. The linings should be compatible, for cleaning purposes, with the top fabrics.

If you would like a skirt with patchwork effect, an apron made of the pieced goods (Figure 10.6) is less work than a whole skirt and can be worn with a number of outfits.

Even smaller applications of patches can be effective. A pocket or yoke can alter the appearance of a top or skirt. For pockets, yokes, or belts, very interesting designs can be made by using triangles instead of squares in the patchwork. To do this, after you have cut out the squares, cut them once more diagonally to make triangles (Figure 10.7).

Now join the triangles to form squares, using different patterned patches on each side.

After you have assembled the triangles back into squares, making sure that each triangle is touching a different pattern, join the squares into rows and the rows into yardage. Then you can cut out the pockets, yokes or belts.

Patchwork fabric also can make very appealing clothes for children, tod-dlers, and even infants. Simply make your squares or triangles smaller, depend-ing on the size of the child, so there is a proper proportion of patchwork to garment.

This type of fabric is not limited to females' clothes, either. Men and boys can also wear patchwork shirts, jackets, shorts, and pants. Nor is there likely to be much difference in the choice of fabrics between men and women; some beauti-ful florals have been used in both men's and women's clothes. The scraps you will use for making these clothes may be of the tailored variety—checks, plaids, stripes—or solids, all types of florals, and provincial prints. Whatever you have, and fashion dictates, can be utilized.

Aside from making your own material out of patches, there are other projects that can utilize leftover scraps. Some of these projects will be suitable for young teenagers who are interested in learning how to sew and would like to begin with simple items which they can actually use when completed.

AN EASY-TO-MAKE TOTE BAG

As an example, the cut-off legs of a pair of jeans or slacks that were cut down into shorts can be converted into an easy-to-make tote bag.

The detailed instructions that follow are written especially to spare mothers from engaging in elaborate sewing lessons. The instructions are for

Fig. 10.7

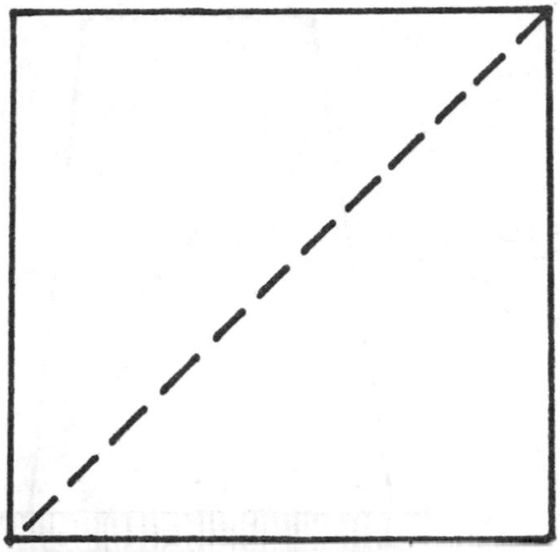

Fig. 10.8

Fig. 10.9

Fig. 10.10

Fig. 10.11

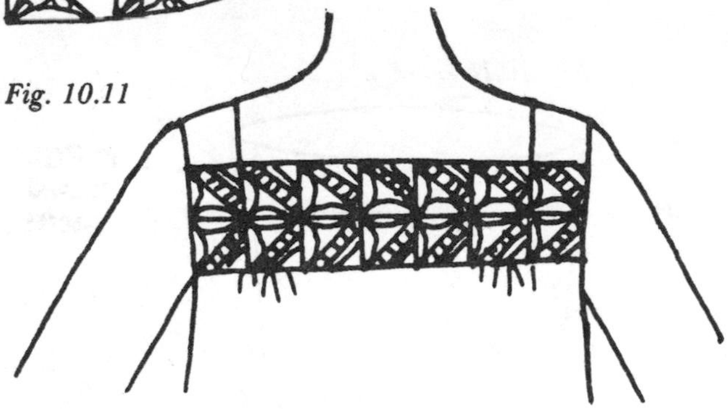

Fig. 10.12

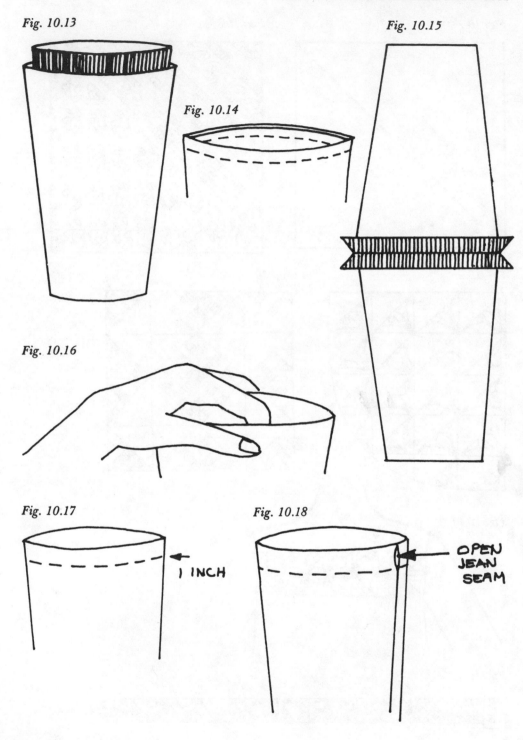

Fig. 10.13

Fig. 10.14

Fig. 10.15

Fig. 10.16

Fig. 10.17

Fig. 10.18

1 INCH

OPEN
JEAN
SEAM

Fig. 10.19

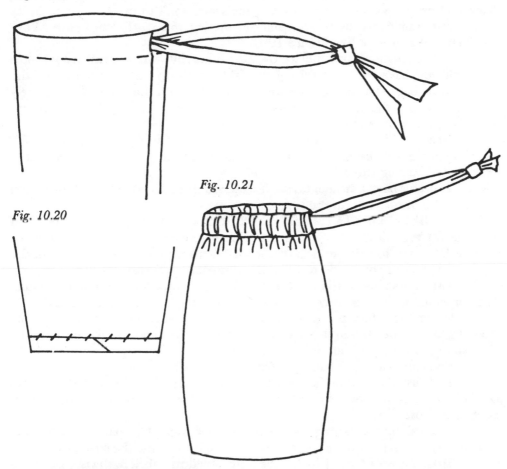

Fig. 10.21

Fig. 10.20

hand sewing in case the family sewing machine cannot be risked on a novice.

The two legs cut off from the jeans or slacks will make up into the tote. The flared bottoms are going to be the top of the bag, and the part where the cut was made will be the bottom.

Measure 16 inches up from the bottom of the jeans legs, make a chalk mark, and cut.

If your jeans have a hem, trim that off. Turn one jean leg inside out. Put the leg that is not turned out inside the other, making sure the flared bottoms are together (Figure 10.13).

Once you have the flared edges together baste them neatly to each other, stitch these two edges together using the combination stitch. This stitch consists of two or three running stitches, then one back-stitch to make the seam stronger. Keep alternating the two or three running stitches with a back-stitch until you complete the seam. (See Figure 10.14.)

When you have stitched all around and come back to your starting point, backstitch in place several times so that the seam won't unravel.

Put your hand inside and pull out the leg you stuffed in before. Your work should now look like Figure 10.15.

Now once more, pull one leg over the other, but with the raw seam inside. You will now have the right side of the fabric both on the outside and on the inside of the bag. The wrong sides will be invisible. With the one half completely folded over the other, find the seam you just made. Press it with your fingers, flattening it as much as you can (Figure 10.16).

Measure 1 inch below this edge and baste all around as in Figure 10.17.

Stitch along the basting, using the combination stitch. When you finish, remove the basting thread.

You now have a tunnel through which to thread a string, rope, or ribbon to make the drawstring on the tote.

But first you need an opening for threading your rope. Look at the top of the tote for the sideseams of the jeans. There will be one on each side. One of them will have no topstitches. Rip that seam down 1 inch—between the top of the tote and the seam you made to form the tunnel. (See Figure 10.18.)

Take the string or ribbon, which should be 1 yard long and no more than ½ inch wide, or the thickness of a pencil; insert a safety pin into one end.

Using the safety pin (closed) as a guide, thread the cord through the opening you made. When it comes through the other end, tie the ends of the drawstring into a firm knot, as in Figure 10.19.

You can close your bag by pulling the cords together.

To finish the bottom of the tote, first baste together the four thicknesses of cloth at the bottom of the bag, making a ½-inch seam. Trim away any uneven spots and loose threads.

Stitch along the basting line, using the backstitch. This part of the bag will bear the weight of the things you put in it, so you have to use the strongest stitch.

Take a woven tape, 1 inch wide and folded in half lengthwise. Cut off a piece 1 inch longer than the bottom of the bag. Fold back the cut edges ½ inch on each end of the tape so the tape is the same length as the bottom. Baste the tape to the bottom, enclosing the raw edge of the bag within the lengthwise fold of the tape.

You should have no raw edges anywhere. Stitch the tape to the bag using the overcast stitch. (See Figure 10.20.)

Voilà—the finished tote!

SLIPPERS FROM SCRAPS

Another simple and useful item for young people to make is a pair of slippers.

Fig. 10.22   *Fig. 10.23*   *Fig. 10.24*

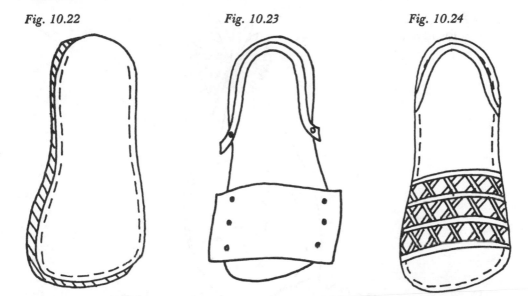

Suitable fabrics would be fake fur, terry cloth from towels, quilted remnants, pieces of felt, or any sturdy fabric, preferably with some thickness. For padding the soles you will need some foam rubber or cardboard.

First, on paper, make outlines of your left and right foot. These will serve as the patterns for the slippers.

From the selected fabric, cut two soles for each foot, ½-inch larger than the pattern outline. That is, you will be allowing a ½-inch seam all around the sole.

Now take the two pieces for the same foot and make a small running stitch ¼ inch from the edge, leaving the heel section unsewn as in Figure 10.22.

From the foam rubber or cardboard, cut out left and right soles exactly to the size of each foot pattern, without any seam allowance.

Insert this piece in the opening you left in the heel section, making a sort of sandwich, with the fabric on top and bottom and the foam or cardboard in the middle. Now stitch up the heel section.

For the top of the slippers, drape a strip of fabric, about 3 inches wide and long enough to go across your instep plus an extra inch. Pin each side to the sole, to get the correct measurement, and cut off extra material, if there is any (Figure 10.23).

At the same time measure a strip of fabric, ½ inch wide, around your ankle from side to side as shown in the illustration.

When you have the correct length of the slipper top and the fabric for the ankle strip, stitch them firmly to the sole where you had them pinned. See Figure 10.24.

Fig. 10.25

FROM THE SMALLEST SCRAPS: A CLOWN DOLL

By now you may be down to smallest scraps of unmatched fabrics. Here is one more idea for the little remnants before you consign them to the garbage bin.

Figure 10.25 shows a clown doll that one of my neighbors makes for her favorite charity. It is a very popular doll and would make a lovely gift for any child. Among its advantages: it uses very small pieces of fabric, the scraps need not be matched, and the sewing is very simple.

About the only thing that is required in large measure is patience.

Besides the fabric, you need two needles, one thin and one thick, and two types of thread, a carpet or heavy-duty thread, and a thin (size 60) thread. The patterns on these pages can be traced on tissue paper.

Figure 10.26 is the clown's hat or hood. (Cut *two* pieces.)

You will also need a clown's face, either bought or homemade, and cotton stuffing (or torn nylon stockings) for the head. (The face can be bought from Lee Wards Creative Crafts Center, 1200 St. Charles Street, Elgin, Illinois 60120.) If you're making the face yourself, you might use a child's sock, stuffed, with features embroidered or painted on. Your arts and crafts store will have a safe and durable paint.

The various scraps you have are to be cut into three sizes of circles: those for body, for arms, and for legs.

Body circles are the size of Figure 10.27. Cut 15 of them.

Leg circles are Figure 10.28. Cut 30 of them.

Arm circles are Figure 10.29. Cut 30, plus one. (The extra arm circle will be used to make a bow tie under the clown's chin after you have sewn on the hood.)

Don't hem any of the circles. Shirr each circle around the edge leaving a ¼ inch seam (Figure 10.30).

Pull the thread in until all the fabric folds over itself and you have a small hole in the middle on the top side of the circle as shown in Figure 10.31.

Keep the different sized circles in separate piles.

Stitch the hood, wrong side out, to the sides of the mask or face as far as the neck. (See Figure 10.32.) Stitch the top of the hood from forehead to point. Use a thin needle and fine thread here.

Turn the hood right side out, back from the face (Figure 10.33).

It will be open at the back from point to bottom. Overlap the open edges, tucking the raw ends inside (Figure 10.34).

Sew the back seam with a small overcast stitch.

Stuff the mask and hood with cotton wadding or old nylon stockings.

Wrap the front neck pieces neatly around the neck, one over the other. Tuck all raw edges inside and stitch to the mask. See Figure 10.35.

If there is too much fabric in the neck pieces, trim some away until it fits neatly.

Take the extra arm circle that you cut and shirred. Now shirr it once more across the center from edge to edge to make a bow (Figure 10.36).

Stitch this bow to the neckband under the chin.

The next step is to make the arms, legs, and body.

Divide the arm circles in half; each arm will have 15 circles.

Take a strong needle—the point must be sharp—and very strong thread, such as carpet thread.

Double the thread and make a firm knot at the end. Sew through the center of the 15 circles (Figure 10.37).

Pull the circles very tightly together and backstitch in place a couple of times.

Turn the needle around and go back again through the center of the 15 circles. Once more, pull the circles tightly together, backstitch in place several times, and cut the thread. Do the same for the other arm.

Sew the 15 large body circles the same way.

Then divide the leg circles, 15 for each leg, and sew them the way you made the arms.

To attach the body to the head, first, take the head and place it on the top circle of the body, right in the center. (See Figure 10.38.)

Now lift up the sides of the two top circles until they touch the bottom of the hood (Figure 10.39).

Sew the lifted edges of the circles to the hood firmly with strong thread. Do the same on both sides.

To attach the arms to the body, first, place the arms against the lifted part of the two top body circles.

Stitch the two top circles of the arms to the lifted part of the two body circles, in the same part where you stitched the body circles to the head. (See Figure 10.40.)

To keep the arms more secure, you can tack the underneath part of the two top arm circles to the third body circle.

To attach the legs, place them on each side of the body under the last body circle.

Sew each leg, with heavy-duty thread, to each half of the two bottom body circles. (See Figure 10.41.) The reason for sewing through two circles instead of one is simply to make it more firm.

If you wish, you can attach a pompom to the ends of each arm and leg and to the top of the hood.

Fig. 10.26

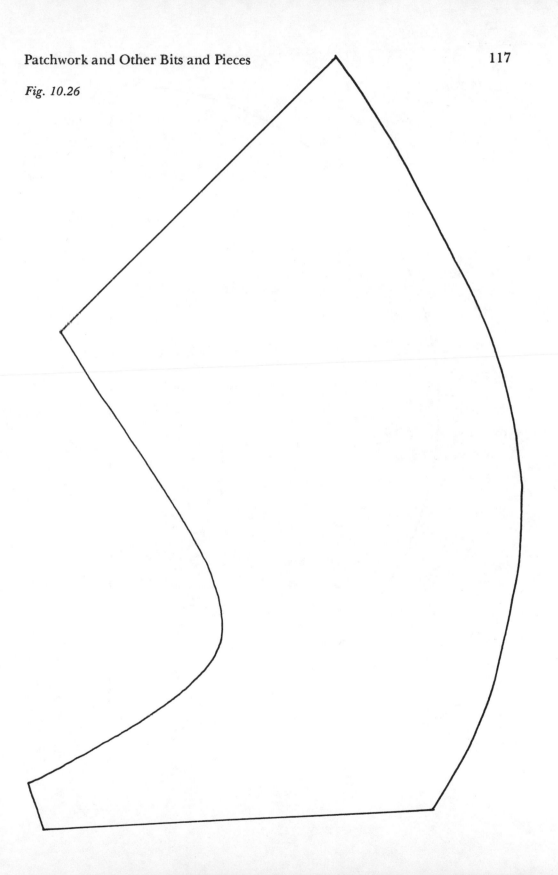

Fig. 10.27 Pattern for half circle

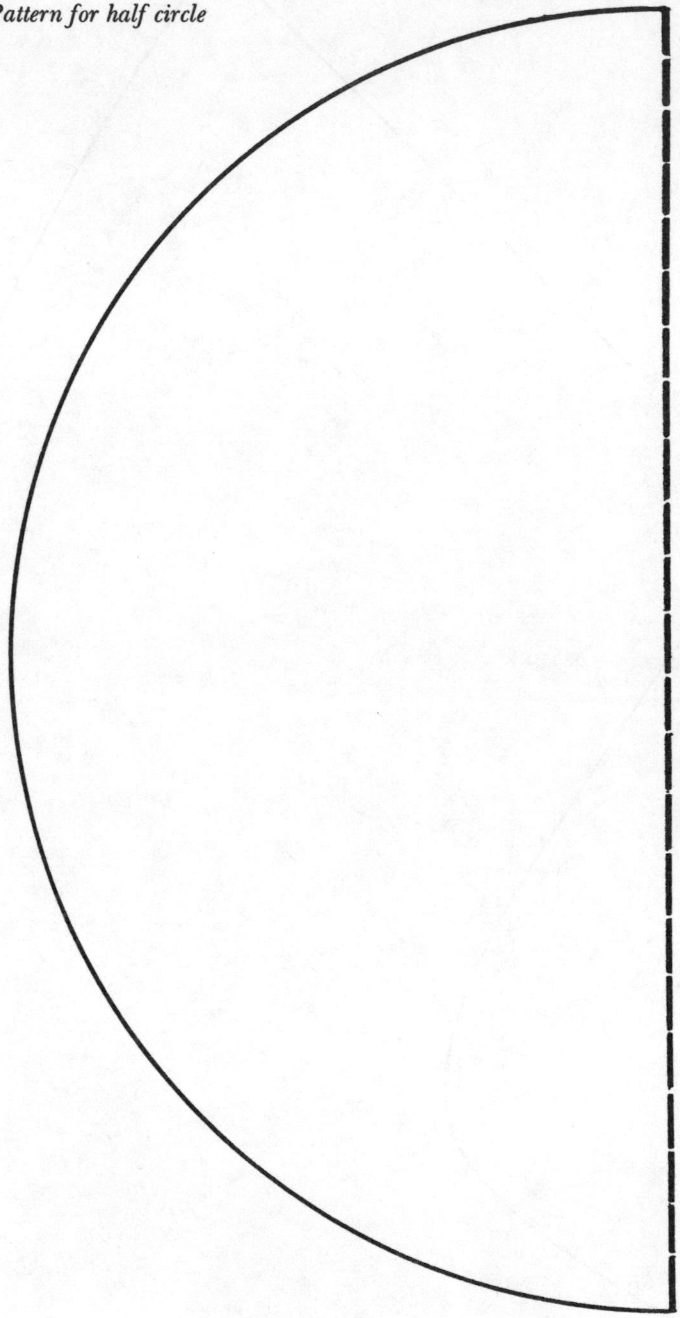

Fig. 10.28

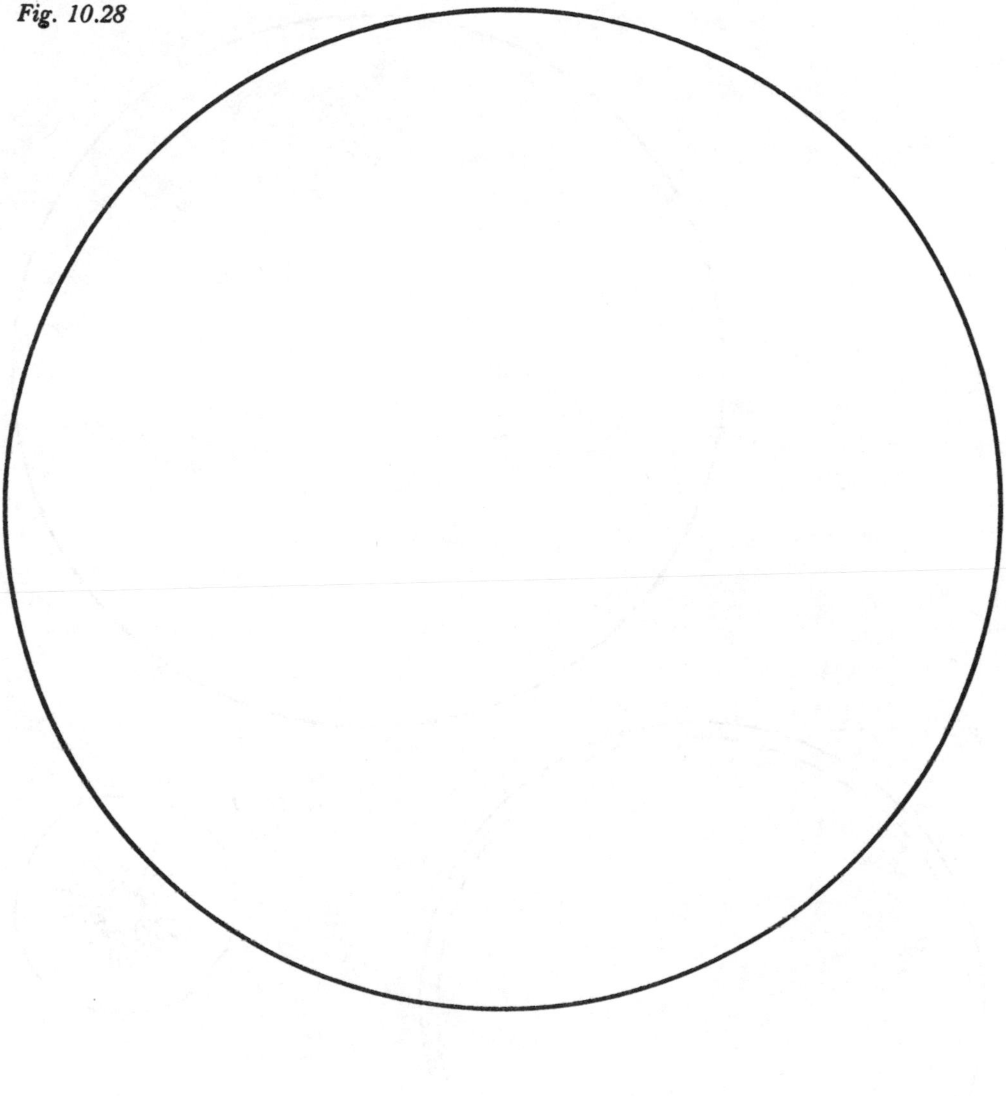

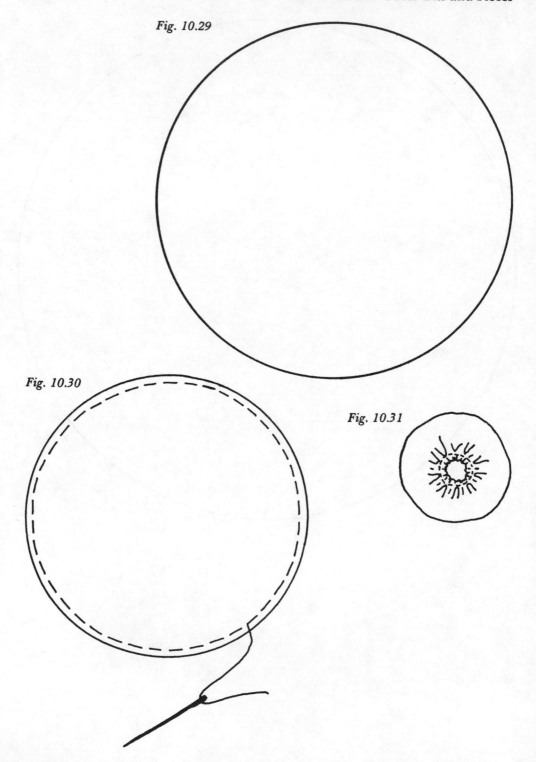

Fig. 10.29

Fig. 10.30

Fig. 10.31

Fig. 10.32

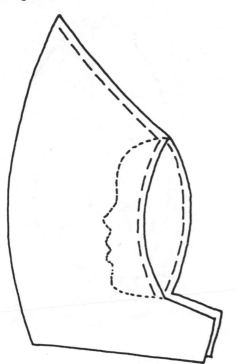

Fig. 10.33

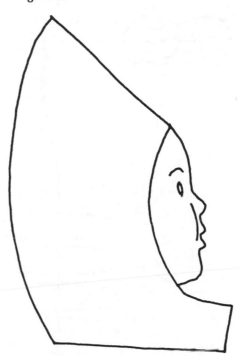

Fig. 10.34

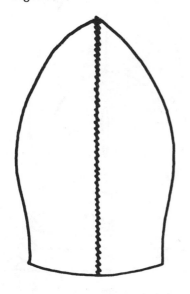

Fig. 10.35

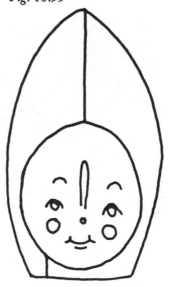

Fig. 10.36   *Fig. 10.37*   *Fig. 10.38*

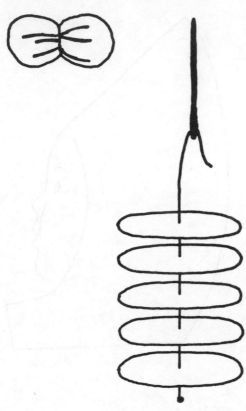

Fig. 10.39

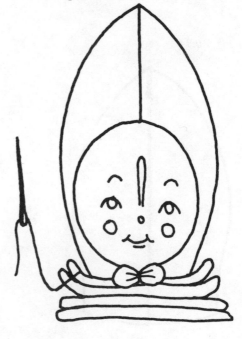

Fig. 10.40

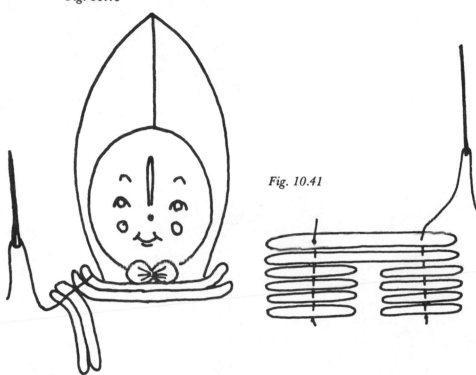

Fig. 10.41

11.
Restyling
with Trimmings

We all have clothes that are both very comfortable and becoming, with the result that we tend to wear them to death. This death can be either imaginary—reflecting boredom—or real—because the fabric has worn itself out in places.

If it's a case of extensively worn or damaged fabric, your garment will go into the recycling pile for whatever use you can make of the still good parts. If it's a small hole or stain, a tastefully chosen trimming can cover up the damage and perhaps restore a favorite garment to useful life.

But if it's simply boredom, trimmings can be used to good advantage to effect some style changes that will give the garment a lift—provided the basic design still is in fashion and the garment fits well.

The most effective places to restyle with trimmings are the sleeves, cuffs, neckline, openings, waist, and hemline. Sometimes a very small change can make a big difference—for instance, an interesting new binding on an existing neckline.

Satin, leather, and suede, real or fake, especially when used on opposite type fabrics—satin on tailored goods, suede on dressy clothes—can produce a dramatically altered appearance. The same binding applied to a neckline can be used to finish off the sleeves as well. However, unless you feel a garment really needs additional emphasis, be careful you don't overdo the trimmings so as not

125

to limit the use of the garment. Begin with one placement at first and add only if you feel it isn't sufficient for the look you are trying to achieve. Also don't forget that a trim must be able to go through the same cleaning process as the rest of the garment.

RESTYLING WITH CUFFS AND OTHER SLEEVE ENDINGS

If you have a dress or blouse with shirt sleeves, a new set of cuffs may make a big change in the look. The fabric to use for the cuffs can be ribbons or lace, or a combination, if you want a soft feminine effect. If the tailored look is desired, it can be a checked napkin or a striped remnant.

As an example, Figure 11.1 shows a vested shirt (or shirtdress) with new cuffs of ribbon and lace.

To make this cuff, first shirr the lace and then stitch the ribbon over the shirring. (See Figure 11.2.) Stitch the cuffs to the sleeves.

Figure 11.3 is a tailored version. The old cuffs that were removed can be used as patterns for the new ones. Sew the new cuffs to the sleeves.

Both of these will be buttoned cuffs. But there are other ways of making cuffs that may be quicker and easier.

Fig. 11.1   *Fig. 11.2*

Fig. 11.3

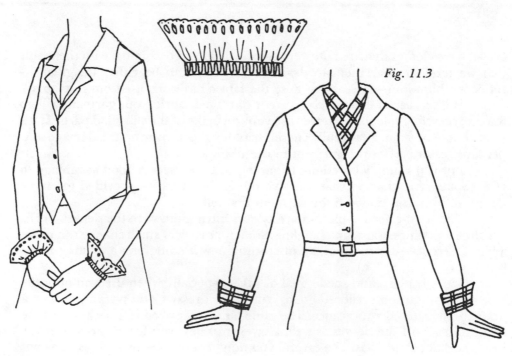

To make the cuff in Figure 11.4, insert a narrow elastic in a casing near the bottom of the sleeve; sew lace or an embroidered trim on the bottom edge.

This makes a pretty sleeve and requires no buttons. If there is a side opening in the sleeve, it can be sewn up. The ruffle can also be made of contrasting fabric, a check, stripe, or print.

All these cuffs can be added to short sleeves as well as to the wrist-length variety. Simply measure around that part of your arm where you want the sleeve to end and make the cuff to fit; don't forget to allow for seams.

Besides cuffs that fit your wrist or arm, other endings for loose-fitting sleeves can be bands, cut straight around the sleeve (Figure 11.5) or flared in a bias cut (Figure 11.6).

If the straight bands are made of ribbon, several different tones of the same color—say from pale pink to deep rose—can change a simple dress into one for a special occasion. The ribbons can be sewed together by overlapping the edges and topstitching, or they can be seamed together on the underside. Similarly, the flared bottom can be made with two layers of flared fabric, one perhaps an embroidered sheer, providing a petticoat effect each time you lift an arm.

Fig. 11.4   *Fig. 11.5*   *Fig. 11.6*

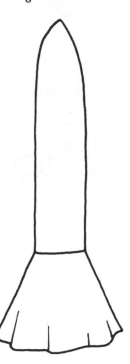

RESTYLING NECKLINES

To give a neckline a fresh look, you can recut it or redecorate it.

Starting with a basic round neckline, here are some possible changes. It is advisable to use either a commercial pattern for a neckline that you like or a pattern you make yourself; pin the pattern onto the original neckline.

Fig. 11.7 Basic round   *Fig. 11.8 Square*   *Fig. 11.9 V neck*

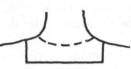

Fig. 11.10 Slash neckline   *Fig. 11.11 U neckline*

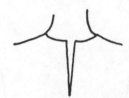
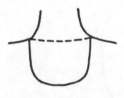

Before you recut a neckline, first remove all the facings. Shoulder seams should be opened a little at the neck to assure a better fit for the new neckline. The opening should be halfway across the shoulder. If there isn't enough material to recut the facings, they can be made of contrasting or lining fabric. The choice will depend on whether the facing shows when the garment is being worn. If it does, a provincial print or a striking contrast can provide the needed lift for a tired dress or blouse.

ADDING COLLARS OR TRIMS

Instead of cutting a new neckline, you can also change an existing one by adding something to it. This can be a collar, piping, or edging.

Starting again with the basic round neck, proceed in the following manner.

Measure around the neckline you wish to change. Use a commercial pattern for the collar, or trace on tissue paper a favorite you may have on another garment, but cut the collar pattern to match the neckline measurement you obtained.

If the dress or blouse opens in the back, slash the back of the collar to correspond with the closing. Allow for a seam on each side of the slash. (Figure 11.12.)

The facings need not be removed from the neckline in order for you to insert the collar. Instead, the collar can be completely finished off with bias tape and slipstitched to the neckline. This is less work and allows for easy removal of the collar if necessary for cleaning or laundering.

Fig. 11.12 Back of collar   Fig. 11.13   Fig. 11.14

 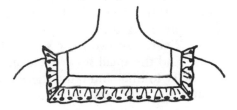

Various styles in collars will suit different necklines. A sailor collar, for example, looks good on a V-neck.

A folded bias strip, 2½ inches wide finished, makes an attractive horseshoe band or a low cowl collar on a U-neck. To make the band fit smoothly, make a small fold in each corner at the front, as in Figure 11.13.

For square necklines, bandings of ribbon, embroidered trims, or braid are all suitable. Pin the trimming around the neck and miter the corners. When everything is in place, topstitch to the dress or blouse.

These bandings can be further embellished by the addition of ruffled edges, as in Figure 11.14. When using this type of edging, first shirr and attach it to the ribbon before applying it to the neckline.

CHANGING AN EXISTING COLLAR

One of the changes that most frequently outdates shirts, blouses, and the like is the shape and size of the collar.

If you have a shirt or a dress on which you would like to change the size or shape of the collar, first rip out the collar, being very careful not to stretch the neckline. Immediately put in a firm machine stitch around the ripped edge of the neck to prevent further stretching while you reshape the collar. If you intend to use the original fabric for the new collar, then the collar should be ripped open and pressed out before recutting it into the new shape. A pattern would help to prevent mistakes; you don't have much material for errors. After sewing up the new collar, place it back into the neckline exactly where the original collar was.

TIES AND SCARVES

Another way to alter the appearance of a neckline or collar is to add a tie or scarf in the same fabric, if you have any, or in a contrast that goes well with the rest of the garment. A pattern traced from a man's tie and cut on the bias will help to achieve a professional finish. Do not stitch the tie to neckline. Knot it under the collar.

Scarves come into fashion often enough to offer a simple solution if other ways of changing the garment's style are not applicable. The scarf material may be obtained from the length or width of the skirt, if the skirt is long or wide enough. If the sleeves are being altered or removed, there may be enough fabric left to piece together into a scarf.

There are two basic shapes for the scarf: the long and narrow (Figure 11.15) and the small square neckerchief (Figure 11.16).

By folding and tying these basic scarves different ways you can achieve a great variety of looks.

Fig. 11.15

Fig. 11.16

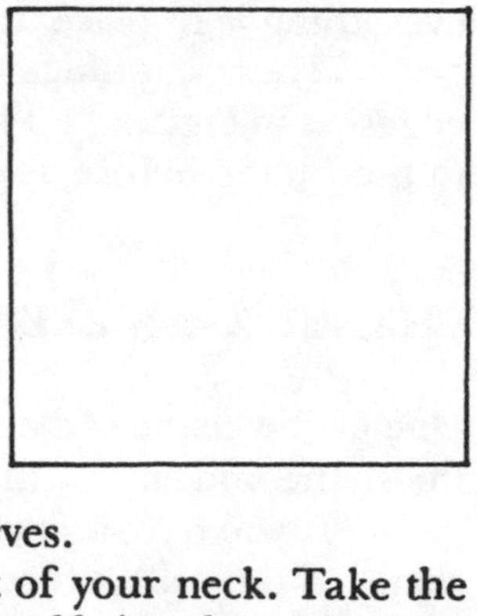

Here are a few ways you can fold and wear scarves.

Place the center of an oblong scarf on the front of your neck. Take the two ends to the back of the neck, cross them at the back and bring the ends again to the front. Loop one end loosely over the other, under the chin. This is an attractive stock tie look.

A skinny oblong scarf looks nice when wrapped to the side of the neck and tied in a knot, the ends left hanging over the shoulder.

A small square scarf can be rolled into a rope and tied around the neck to look like a necklace. A gold or silver chain can be wrapped around the scarf rope to further the illusion of a necklace. This scarf can be tied center front.

Fold a large square on the bias and tie around the neck with a knot in the back. This will form a cowl neckline in the front. If the square is large, the cowl will be soft and low on the neck. With a small square the bias folds will be high on the neck.

For evening wear, a large, long chiffon or silk scarf can be thrown across the front of the neck and shoulders with the ends trailing in the back.

RESTYLING GARMENT CLOSINGS

Closings offer other opportunities for updating the styling of a favorite garment.

The easiest change is a new set of buttons, say, gold or silver or some type of novelty button replacing color-matched or fabric-covered ones. More interesting effects can be achieved, however, by altering the method of closing the dress or top. In this case the buttons are removed and the buttonholes cut away. The replacement can be whatever is in current fashion: ties sewn on each side of the closing, novelty zippers, or frogged buttonholes and buttons looped in the Chinese manner.

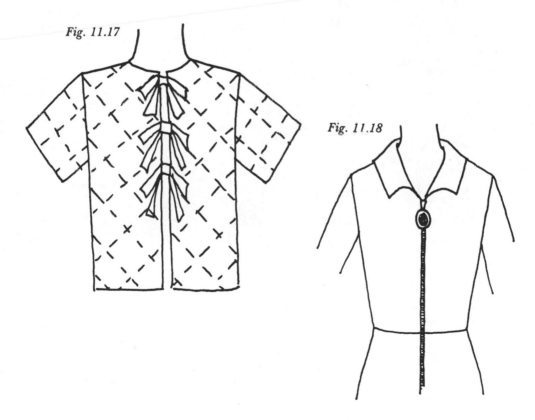

Fig. 11.17

Fig. 11.18

Fig. 11.19

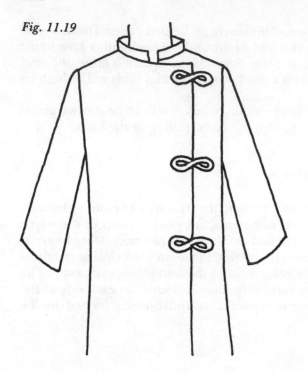

Fig. 11.20   *Fig. 11.21*   *Fig. 11.22*

Fig. 11.23

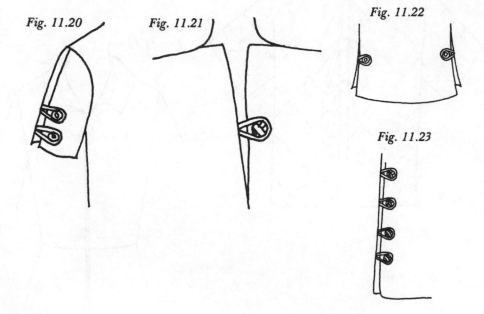

In Figure 11.17 the back zipper of the overblouse was removed and the seam sewn up. The center front was slit open and faced out with contrasting fabric. The same fabric was used to make the piping that formed the ties. These were stitched on each side of the opening to ½-inch from the edge. They could have been inserted into the facing but then the ends wouldn't have tied as closely together.

Figure 11.18 shows a shirtwaist type of dress. The buttons and buttonholes, together with the strips of fabric to which they had been attached, were cut away. A ¼-inch seam was left on for a facing. A novelty zipper was inserted up to the point where the buttons previously ended.

Figure 11.19 represents a side closure on a jacket. Originally there were heavy-duty covered snaps. These were left in place to keep the opening from shifting. Chinese frogs with matching buttons, all made of braid, were sewn on top for a decorative effect.

Instead of removing buttons, you might try adding them on in unexpected places. My favorite areas are slits, wherever they occur. On sleeves, necklines, or hems of tops and dresses, loops and buttons add a decorative touch.

For any garment closing where a zipper would be used, that is, where the edges of the garment simply meet rather than overlap, there is another form of closing which can give interesting casual or dressy effects. On each side of the closing eyelets can be made (and then stitched or embroidered to prevent raveling), or "punched-in" with the inexpensive metal eyelet kits available. The eyelets can then be laced up with decorative laces, yarn, etc. A simpler and surer way to add metal eyelets might be to ask your local shoe repair man to put them in; he can add eyelets or "grommets" easily even to heavy fabrics and leather.

RESTYLING WAISTLINES AND HEMLINES

Waist and hemlines are two other places where freshening changes can be made.

For the waist, a new belt can alter the look of a dress and bring it in line with current fashion. This, of course, varies from year to year, or, more accurately, from season to season.

For example, if a dress has a narrow self belt, a wide obi sash can alter the style dramatically. The sash can be very interesting if made of long strips of different fabrics, perhaps left over from hems of other dresses and from remnants (See Figure 11.24).

Discarded men's ties, wide or narrow, can also be used as belts. Some of these have sensational colors and patterns. Measure the tie to fit your waist, and add 3 inches. Cut off the rest of the tie. Attach a pull-through buckle to the cut end.

Also, since men's ties are made of bias fabric, they can be made into excellent luxurious bias strips for trimming the edges of garments, wherever their colors and designs would be appropriate. Simply cut the ties into lengthwise strips.

Ribbons are another source of attractive belts. They can be stitched to a firm backing and finished with gold- or silver-colored pull-through buckles found at notions counters. Figure 11.25 shows a belt made of embroidered ribbon.

And, finally, a garment can be updated by removing the belt altogether. This works very effectively with a flared tent-cut dress or top, like the dress in Figure 11.26. Don't forget to remove the belt guides when you do this.

As for the hems, even if they don't need lengthening or shortening, there are numerous ways of enlivening them.

For example, you can scallop the bottom and use a bright print for lining the scallops as shown in Figure 11.27

Or, you can attach a lace trim or ruffle on the inside of the dress for a lingerie look (Figure 11.28). Tack it to the hem binding. This will show when you walk or sit.

Periodically, a fur-bordered hem becomes fashionable. This is the time to use that old fur piece, real or pretend, that is too good to throw away, but not good enough to wear. See Chapter 5 for complete instructions for making and attaching fur hems.

You might try this on a culotte worn above boots (Figure 11.29) if you'd like to stop traffic.

Fig. 11.24 Obi

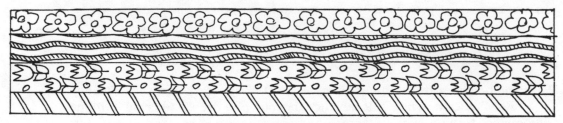

Fig. 11.25 Embroidered ribbon

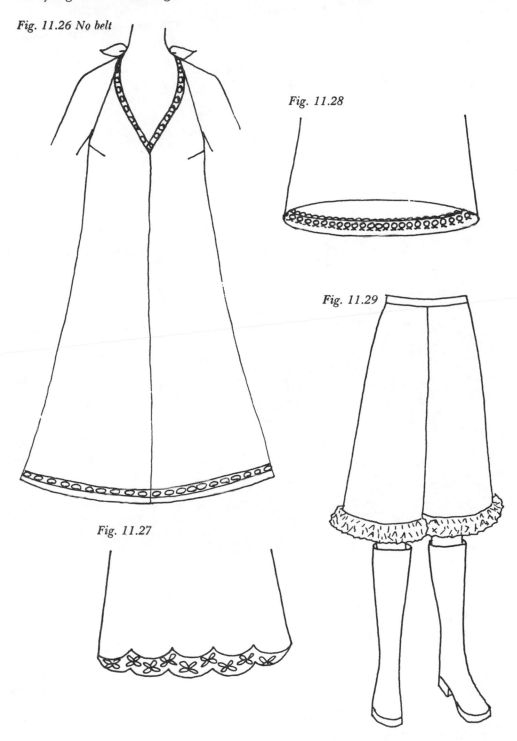

Fig. 11.26 No belt

Fig. 11.28

Fig. 11.29

Fig. 11.27

12.
Reviving Clothes with Decorative Stitchery and Trims

Embroidery, quilting, appliqués, and other forms of needlework are major crafts in themselves, and there are many books devoted to each one. This chapter is focused on how to use decorative stitchery to brighten up or revive recycled clothes.

To do this, though, some knowledge of the basic stitches is necessary. So before discussing their use, let's look at some of the simplest and most frequently used stitches.

The running stitch. This is a stitch we associate with basting. (See Figure 12.1.) For decorative purposes every stitch should be of equal length. The length of the top stitch is usually twice that of the one underneath, but it can vary as long as all the top stitches are the same length and all the underneath stitches are also even.

The backstitch. Here the underside stitch is twice the length of the top stitch. Also the top stitches start next to each other, with no space left between them (Figure 12.2). This is done by bringing the needle, after it emerges on the topside, back to the hole of the previous stitch.

The satin stitch. These are stitches of even length worked side by side closely together as shown in Figure 12.3.

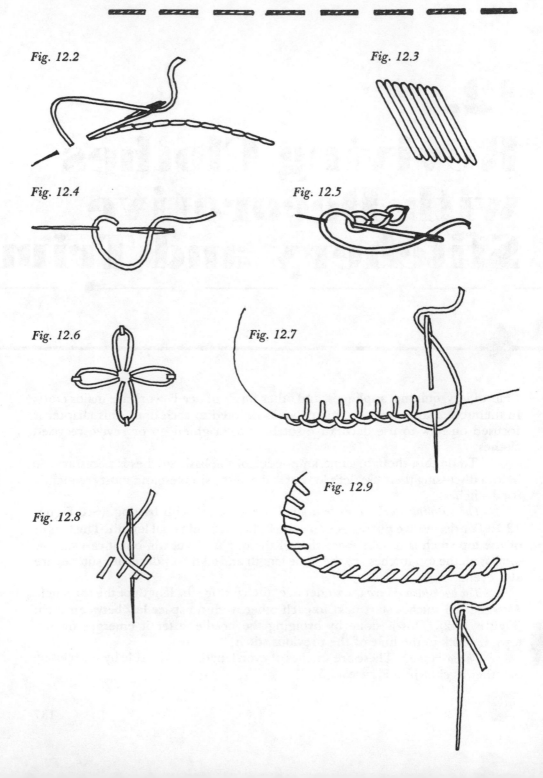

Fig. 12.1

Fig. 12.2

Fig. 12.3

Fig. 12.4

Fig. 12.5

Fig. 12.6

Fig. 12.7

Fig. 12.8

Fig. 12.9

The chain stitch. The chain stitch is a looped stitch. Make a stitch of whatever length desired. When the point of the needle emerges on the topside of the fabric, loop the thread under the needle point before pulling the needle through completely (Figure 12.4). This forms the loop. After pulling the needle through, start the next stitch just on the outside of the newly formed loop. Keep all the loops the same size. (See Figure 12.5.)

The lazy daisy stitch. This is a single chain stitch, often four or five of them are grouped as a flower. In Figure 12.6 each petal is a single chain stitch.

The buttonhole stitch. This is a looped stitch usually sewn around an edge (Figure 12.7). The stitches can be spaced wide apart or placed very close together, both for design purposes and to keep cloth from unraveling.

The cross-stitch. This is another easy-to-do stitch. A fabric that has a small check woven into it, such as gingham, is ideal for this type of embroidery since it provides a guide for the stitches. And a material like piqué is good because it has defined "squares" in the weave. Bring the needle and thread up from bottom left to top right of the check, working a row rather than single crosses. At the end of the row come back by bringing the needle from bottom right to top left, crossing every check. (See Figure 12.8.)

The overcast stitch. This stitch is frequently used in appliqués to cover raw edges. (See Figure 12.9.) Bring the needle up close to the edge of the fabric. Loop the needle and thread over the edge and bring it up next to the first hole. Continue until you cover all the raw edges.

These stitches have many variations, but for use in recycling clothes, the basic versions will serve just as well and are easier to master.

DECORATING WITH APPLIQUÉS

Actually, many appealing decorations require no special stitches. Appliqués can be put on by machine or by hand with a small overcast stitch. The outstanding attraction in an appliqué is the design and how well it fits in with the garment it is being applied to.

Another advantage to decorating with appliqués is that they are equally appropriate for jeans and evening wear, a child's dress or a pot holder. (Not necessarily the same appliqué, of course.)

You can cut out floral or geometric motifs of print remnants and apply them to clothes that need some brightening rather than alteration.

When cutting out a design, leave a ¼-inch seam all around. The seam allowance should be turned under like a hem and pressed before applying to the garment.

If the grain of the appliqué fabric is in the same direction as that of the garment cloth, there is less chance of puckering. Before sewing the appliqué to the garment, baste it in place first. With a hemmed appliqué a small overcast stitch can be used to sew it.

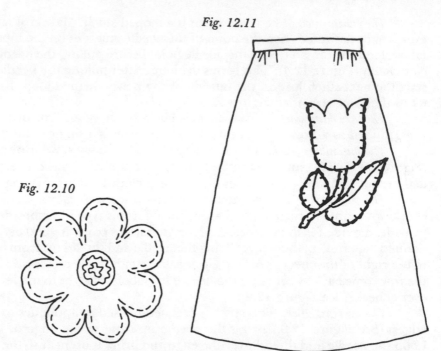

Fig. 12.11

Fig. 12.10

When the appliqué has too many tiny edges to turn back even a small seam allowance, one of the embroidery stitches becomes necessary. This can be either a small overcast stitch Figure 12.9 or a close buttonhole stitch Figure 12.7.

If you feel sufficiently proficient in the use of these stitches, a contrasting embroidery thread can add something extra. However, if you are uncertain of your needlecraft skills, a thread to match the background of the design will hide unintentional variations in stitches.

The appliqué need not be a ready-made motif. It can be something of your own design and in solid colors. First draw the design on paper and transfer it to cloth the way you transfer darts from a commercial pattern with a tracing wheel. Here, again, leave ¼-inch hem everywhere to bend under. Designing your own appliqués leaves room for imaginative use of leftover scraps. The petals of a flower, for example, can be of different colors; and a bird or animal appliqué can be made from an unconventional plaid or patchwork.

Commercial patterns carry designs for appliqués as well as embroidery transfers for those who prefer to work with them. However, any design that appeals to you can be traced or adapted from pictures, photographs, and illustrations that appear in magazines, newspapers, and other widely available sources.

Another interesting treatment of appliqués is to puff them out a bit if they're going into places where the slight bulge won't matter. For this you shape a thin layer of filling, a trifle smaller than the design and without a seam allowance. A polyester fiberfill, carried in fabric stores and at five-and-tens, makes an excellent filling for most fabrics. Baste the filling to the underside of the appliqué before turning under the seams of the top fabric. After the seams are basted and pressed, they will sandwich the filling and the design can be applied as previously described.

When making designs for children's clothing, an appliqué can form a pocket if it is first lined and the top part isn't stitched to the garment. See Figure 12.11. To line the pocket, cut a lining exactly the same shape as the appliqué. Stitch ¼ inch seam around the edge on the wrong side, leaving an opening of 1½ inches so that the appliqué can be turned right side out. Sew up the opening, tucking the raw edges inside. Lining the appliqué will give it more body to serve as a pocket. Sew the pocket on each side and bottom to the garment, leaving the top part unattached.

DECORATING WITH TRAPUNTO

A decoration similar to quilting but involving less work, and more suitable for small areas, is called trapunto. Here a motif is outlined with a running stitch.

For trapunto work you will need some lining material and a thin layer of filling. The filling is the kind used in quilting, polyester or cotton, and the backing can be of either cotton or rayon. (It is a good idea to make all your decorations, including linings and fillers, washable if the garment that's being decorated is washable.)

In trapunto nothing goes on the top side of the fabric except the running stitch. The design comes from outlining some part of a print or, in case of a solid color fabric, inventing a design of your own with the running stitch. See Figure 12.12. The easiest way to see your design on both the outside and the inside of the garment is to outline it with a contrasting thread using the basting stitch. This thread will be pulled out after you finish the design.

Pin or baste the filler and then the lining over the filler on the underside of the garment, covering the whole area that will be outlined and extending a little beyond.

The thread for the trapunto should match the background color of the fabric; this will make the finished design more effective in a subtle way than if a contrasting thread is used. Sew the running stitch on the topside of the fabric following the design.

Another way of working a trapunto design is to use a cord instead of a filler. The cord should be fairly soft, the kind used in upholstery cording. The width will depend on what effect you wish to achieve. This treatment is good for hems, sleeves, and necklines.

Place the cord on the underside of the garment and over it a strip of lining, basting everything in place. It is easiest to make plain straight lines, but a simple design can be worked out. Work the running stitch on the topside of the

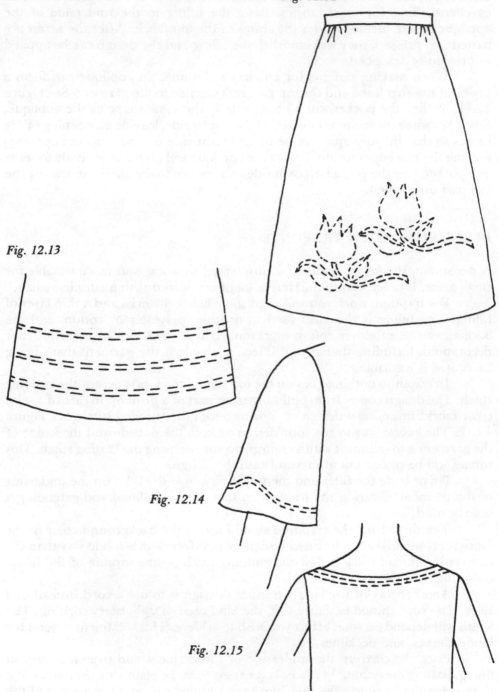

Fig. 12.12

Fig. 12.13

Fig. 12.14

Fig. 12.15

garment, guiding the needle alongside the cord with your fingers. First stitch along one side of the cord, after you finish one side then along the other side. The stitching goes through the lining as well, forming a casing around the cord.

This type of decoration is used mostly for adult clothing and some household articles. It is considered somewhat sophisticated for children's apparel, where an appliqué would give a brighter touch.

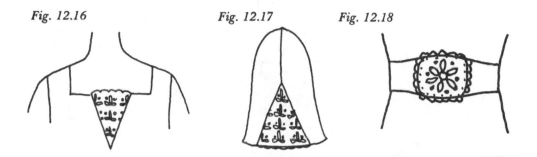

Fig. 12.16   Fig. 12.17   Fig. 12.18

DECORATING WITH EMBROIDERY

Embroidery would be used more frequently than it is if it weren't thought of in terms of a major project. However, that needn't be so.

For example, a couple of daisies on a collar or cuffs can add fresh appeal to a blouse or dress. As previously noted, these daisies need be nothing more than a cluster of single lazy daisy stitches in a flower arrangement.

Or a touch of embroidery can be combined with an appliqué, such as an embroidered stem or leaf on an appliqué apple.

By keeping your decorations confined to areas that can be removed and changed—pockets, belts, cuffs—you can experiment a bit until you accomplish the look you wish to create.

If you want to use embroidery but don't trust yourself making it, look over retired embroidered clothing as well as old hankies, small napkins, and other unused linens to see what can be converted into insertions of appliqués. The insertions can be made at neckline, sleeves, waistline, and somewhere in the skirt, depending on the style.

Sometimes a decorative stitch can be suggested rather than carried out in the traditional manner. If you are recycling a garment that has puffed sleeves or a full skirt, you might consider the illusion of smocking.

On the sleeve every inch or so, you can pinch together three small tucks, about ½ inch long, and catch them several times with an overcast stitch. This is shown in Figures 12.19 and 12.20.

The trim need not be carried all around the arm. The top part of the sleeve will suffice.

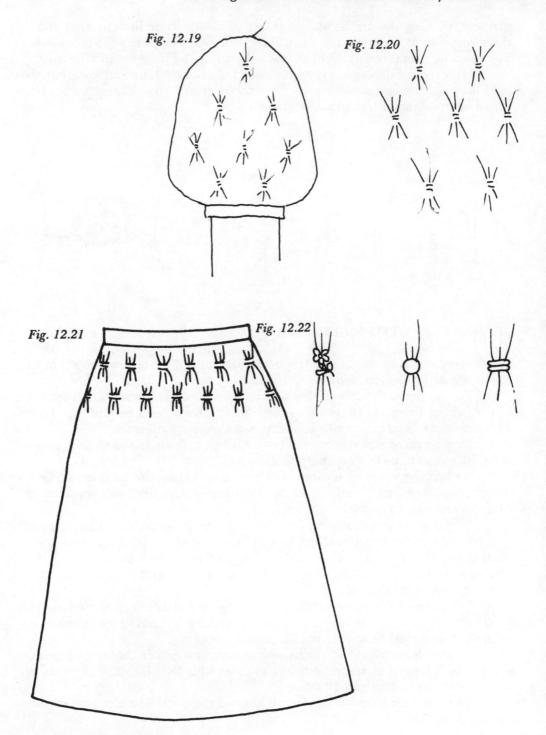

Fig. 12.19

Fig. 12.20

Fig. 12.21

Fig. 12.22

When you use this trim on a skirt, you can either make a few rows from the waist down, or cover the whole skirt, provided it's full enough.

A more elaborate way of using this decoration is to add a bead or a tiny fabric flower—a violet or lily of the valley with or without a stem—when catching the tucks with the thread. The flower or bead is sewn on with the same stitches that hold the tucks together (Figure 12.22).

This decorative treatment is especially effective with sheer fabrics and can transform a simple dirndl skirt or a dress with a gathered skirt into a special-occasion garment at very little or no cost.

DECORATING WITH BEADS AND SEQUINS

Periodically, beads and sequins become fashionable. While they do suggest formal and dressy clothes, this does not necessarily have to be the case. Wooden or chalk beads can decorate casual garments with great flair. Sequins are frequently used on children's theatrical play costumes as well as adult evening wear.

The easiest way to apply them is to buy ready-made motifs and edgings. However, if you are determined to do it all yourself, the simplest method is to use the running stitch, threading the beads each time the needle emerges topside. You can work out a design or simply make rows of beads across the garment. If you have a flowered dress or blouse, you can outline a few flowers in beads at neckline or sleeves for a dressier look. Generally beaded garments must be dry-cleaned.

Fig. 12.23

DECORATING WITH SELF-FABRIC FLOWERS

A flower made from the same fabric as the dress or blouse it decorates, is one of my favorite fashion accents. Fabric flowers can be works of art, but a simple one, a daisy or a rosebud, is not difficult to do and will accomplish the same effect as a more complicated one.

Fig. 12.24

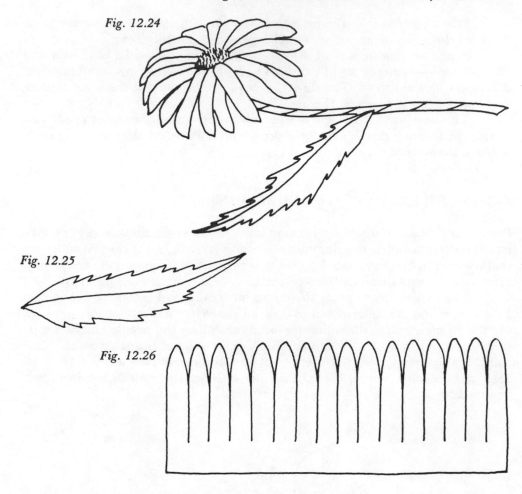

Fig. 12.25

Fig. 12.26

Fig. 12.27

Fig. 12.28

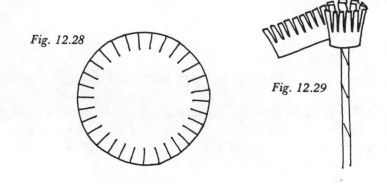

Fig. 12.29

To make a daisy you need a strip of fabric 5 inches long, 1¾ inches wide, for the petals; a strip 3½ inches long, ½ inch wide for the stamens; a circle 1¼ inches in diameter for calyx; 2 strips, each 3 inches long, ¼ inch wide, to cover the stem; a leaf (Figure 12.25) cut out free hand to approximate a daisy leaf.

You will also need some starch to stiffen the fabric, a glue that dries colorless, such as Sobo available at craft stores, and a few inches of florist's wire for the stem (I use wired ties that come with plastic bags). Now you are ready to proceed. First starch the fabric before cutting it into shapes. Mix a tablespoon of cornstarch in ¾ cup of water, cook till it thickens, then add a tablespoon of the "Sobo" or similar glue, stir and cool. Spread the mixture on the back of the fabric, keeping it flat, and let it dry. When dry, cut the pieces for the flowers. Take the petal strip and serrate one of the long sides with pinking shears. Make slits along the serrated side, 2/3 of the way into the fabric (Figure 12.26).

Cut slits on one long side of the stamen piece (Figure 12.27) and around the calyx (Figure 12.28).

Spread glue on the back of one of the narrow strips for the stem. Wrap it diagonally around the top half of the wire (or stiffened tie). Spread glue on the back of the unslit side of the stamen strip. Wrap it neatly around the top of the stem.

After you slash the petals, they will likely curve back of their own accord. You can help them do that by pressing them back with the blunt edge of a knife that has been heated. Heat only the part of the knife you will use to press back the petals. Use a pot holder to hold the knife. Gather the uncut side of the petal strip with needle and thread until the circumference will go around the glued stamens without overlapping.

Apply the glue to the gathered edge of the petals and press them around the stamens.

Make a hole in the center of the calyx with a sharp object, put glue on the inside part and slide it up the stem to cup the bottom of the flower. Put glue on the bottom of the leaf and wrap it around the stem where you ended the first stem strip. Now glue the back of the second stem strip and wrap the rest of the stem including the bottom of the leaf to attach it firmly to the stem.

The leaf, calyx, and stem pieces can be cut of green fabric, to give the natural look, if desired. However, the entire flower can be made of the same material as the garment it decorates, for the custom-made effect. The flower should be removed for cleaning or washing purposes.

You can design other flowers by copying the natural petals. All fabrics must be stiffened first as described in the instructions for the daisy. Heated utensils—the blunt edge of a knife or the cup of a spoon—are used to press the petals into curves and shapes. Any material used in clothing is suitable for artificial flowers.

Glossary

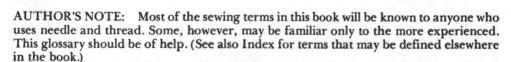

AUTHOR'S NOTE: Most of the sewing terms in this book will be known to anyone who uses needle and thread. Some, however, may be familiar only to the more experienced. This glossary should be of help. (See also Index for terms that may be defined elsewhere in the book.)

F.C.

Appliqué. A small piece of fabric forming some kind of decorative motif, which is stitched on to a garment.

Bias tape. A fabric tape cut on the diagonal, therefore having a lot of stretch.

Bind. To finish an edge by sewing a strip of fabric to both sides of it.

Capelet. A small cape, often covering the armholes of a garment only (rather than the entire shoulders).

Casing. A strip of fabric stitched, along both its edges, to a garment. The two ends of the strip are left open to insert an elastic or some other tie that can be pulled through.

Dart. A small, stitched fold, usually triangular, to make a garment fit better.

Dirndl. A skirt which is gathered at the waist.

Ease. To fit a larger piece of pattern into a smaller one by very slightly gathering in the extra fullness. This can be done only with a small amount of extra fabric.

Face out. To apply a facing.

Facings. Pieces of fabric sewn to the garment edges that are not attached to other parts of the garment nor finished off by hemming. Facings serve to hide raw edges and to give additional body—necklines, sleeves, hems, front openings. A facing is usually about 2 inches wide.

Hem allowance. The extra fabric needed for a hem, usually 2 inches for the bottom of a dress or skirt, 1 inch for bottom of a sleeve. This varies with the style and fabric.

Overlap. To bring one edge of a garment over its opposite edge. This is done most frequently to provide space for closing, such as buttons and buttonholes.

Passementerie. A trimming of braid stitched into some design, usually sold by the yard, occasionally by units such as medallions.

Piping. A bias tape, usually folded over the entire length. Sometimes the raw edges are pressed to the inside of the fold, ready to apply to the garment. Available at most notion counters.

Seam allowance. The fabric needed to sew a seam. Most seams are stitched ½ inch from the edge and this ½ inch is the seam allowance.

Self fabric. The major fabric used in a garment, from which accessories and trims are often made.

Selvage. The finished edge of fabric as it comes from the mill or store; this is the edge (or edges) that runs along the length of the fabric.

Shirr. To gather the fabric for control of fullness, as in a dirndl skirt or a puffed sleeve.

Topstitching. Stitches made on, and visible on, the surface of the fabric of a garment (as opposed to "inside" or seam stitching).

Tubing. The same as casing, a strip of fabric sewn onto a garment for threading elastic, ribbon, or some other tie. Tubing can also be formed by bending back an inch or so of an edge and stitching it down, leaving a small opening for threading a tie. This is the customary method for making a drawstring waist on skirt or pants.

Tuck (n). A small fold of fabric, either stitched down or simply caught in a seam. The stitched version is usually for decoration and style, whereas a tuck in a seam is to control a little fullness.

Tuck (v). To make tucks.

Tunnel. Same as tubing.

Index